NORTHERN PASSAGES

NORTHERN PASSAGES

*Reflections from
Lake Superior Country*

Michael Van Stappen

Illustrations by Kate Wright

PRAIRIE OAK PRESS
Madison, Wisconsin

First edition, first printing.
Copyright © 1998 by Michael Van Stappen
Illustrations copyright © 1998 by Kate Wright

Prairie Oak Press
821 Prospect Place
Madison, Wisconsin 53703

Typeset by Quick Quality Press, Madison, Wisconsin
Designed by Prairie Oak Press
Printed in the United States of America by
Thomson-Shore, Inc., Dexter, Michigan
Cover illustration by Kate Wright

The essays "A Superior Wilderness," "In Praise of Yellow Birch," "Blueberry Roads," "Ephemeral, Like Clouds," "Old Copper," and "On the Trail of Wolves" first appeared in *Country Journal.* "A Fine Madness" and "The Steelhead God" first appeared in *Wisconsin Outdoor Journal.* The versions of most of these essays have been revised by the author to appear in this book.

Library of Congress Cataloging-in-Publication Data

Van Stappen, Michael
Northern passages: reflections from Lake Superior country /
Michael Van Stappen; illustrations by Kate Wright.—1st ed.
    p.   cm.
ISBN 1-879483-40-8 (alk. paper)
1. Natural history—Wisconsin—Anecdotes. 2. Natural history—
Michigan—Upper Peninsula—Anecdotes. 3. Van Stappen, Michael.
I. Title.
QH105.W6V35 1998
508.775'1—dc21
                                           98-17055
                                              CIP

*This book is for Julie,
Jessica and Casey,
and for family and friends
both near and far.*

CONTENTS

NORTHERN PASSAGES

THE FORGOTTEN LAND

One early spring morning I drove far down the slushy back roads to an old riveted steel bridge that had been built sometime between the two world wars. Along the way, I could see that winter's blanket of snow was quickly melting away. The weather had recently been unseasonably seasonal, which is to say that early spring weather in Lake Superior country has all the predictability of an earthquake, and sometimes a similar, though milder, effect on our lives. But for the past few weeks the sun had shone more or less reliably and the few rain showers that had fallen were warm. The snowy upland fields and pastures were already revealing patches of pale, matted grasses and weeds. Small flocks of sparrows could be seen setting down in some of these fresh openings to feed upon fallen seeds remaining from last autumn.

The engineers who designed the bridge placed it a short distance downstream from the confluence of Pine and North Fish Creeks. At the bridge, I leaned over a rusty riveted rail and watched a boiling brown slurry of water, ice, mud, branches, and twigs, rushing madly beneath the bridge. Above the water's roar, every so often I heard strange, dull thuds. These were most likely the sounds of large stones or small boulders smacking other rocks as they grudgingly tumbled along the bottom, levered downstream by the sheer force of high spring flow.

Peering downstream, I began to see how North Fish Creek had etched itself into this steep-sided valley of its own making. Melting snow and rainwater from fields and forests hundreds of feet above funnel down into countless small ravines. These in turn lead to larger ravines which finally empty into the creek. Once the snow starts melting and spring rains begin to fall, it doesn't take long for all this water to find the creek. In a matter of days, this humble stream crescendos to a torrent, carving its way ever deeper into the landscape.

If glacial geologists are right, it seems the life of North Fish Creek must have started about 8500 years ago. At this time, a great lobe of the Wisconsin glacial ice sheet, which had covered this area for thousands of years, began to melt and recede. Geologists called it the Chippewa Lobe. As this immense, decaying ice sheet withdrew, several lakes formed in its wake. These were bound on the north by the wasting ice front and on the south by the Penokee highlands. As the glacier continued retreating, these lakes grew in size, eventually joining together as one great lake that geologists have named Glacial Lake Duluth. As the ice continued retreating northward into what is now Canada, the surface level of this Lake Duluth began falling in stages. Eventually it reached a level close to that of modern day Lake Superior.

Here along the North Coast a new landscape born of ice and water had emerged. Most of the lowlands, formerly glacial lake bottoms, were covered deeply with iron-rich clay that came from the melting glacier. Ancient sand beaches formed in places along the shorelines of these glacial lakes. These beaches are not uncommon and can be found at elevations up to five hundred feet or so above present day Lake Superior. Stands of oaks and pines on hillsides and dry soil flowers like fringed polygala and trailing arbutus offer strong hints of their presence.

Above the reach of the glacial lakes, the broad highland that runs the length of the Bayfield Peninsula was more directly shaped by the receding ice front. Here the dry, sandy land reads like a text-book of glacial features: kettles and potholes, recessional moraines, pitted outwash plains, braided streambeds. It is a land apart from the rest, with dry forests and openings that are prone to fire, and a topography that defies common sense to all but geologists. These unique features are the very underpinning of the unique ecosystems we call the barrens. It is difficult enough to comprehend—much less believe it possible—that such a parched landscape was born of ice and water.

Most of us living here today are oblivious to the epic drama out of which Lake Superior and the North Coast country was reborn. It was a rebirth not by fire but by ice—a horrendous rending and reshaping of a new landscape by the vast and distant energies of the atmosphere and oceans. Evidence of this great rebirth is everywhere underfoot. It is the very underpinning of our existence here today. To see it, we need only to look.

Steelhead fishing was the ostensible reason for my visit to North Fish Creek that day. But the water was much too high and the wonder too deep to think about fishing. I went home happily empty-handed, my head churning like the river with images and ideas.

The next year I returned to the creek a week later in the spring, again to fish for steelhead. My timing was lucky, because the high water had already passed and a good flow still remained for all the fish heading upstream to spawn. Outfitted in my floppy green chest waders (which I now realize were designed to leak) and lucky felt fishing hat, I crossed the bridge and waltzed through a thicket of mixed alders and willow shoots. As I moved downstream, I looked for bigger pools where resting fish might hang out.

Coming around one particular bend, I found a beautiful swirling pool at the bottom of a fast moving riffle. The pool was beyond reach from shore so I waded across shallow water to some boulders and fished from there. After ten minutes without a bite, I decided to move downstream. Instead of backtracking, I took a shortcut off the rocks, stepping onto what looked like solid sand.

That step was a big mistake. Within seconds I was over my knees in what turned out to be quicksand, and I was sinking fast. I felt like a bug stuck on flypaper, a mastodon going down for the last count in the tar pits. I tossed my favorite fly rod ashore, thinking at least the rod would be saved, and maybe searchers would know where to grapple for the body.

But I had no desire to become a fossil, at least not yet. Writhing and straining and cursing, slowly I unscrewed myself and, still in possession of waders, crawled to terra firma. Resting there dolefully, full of mud and sand, I realized the patch of quicksand had probably formed over the last few weeks when the creek had been much higher. A light mix of mud, sand, air, and water had been deposited in an eddy on my side of the big pool. The water level went down, the surface dried a little, and a natural trap was set.

After gathering my gear, I hiked farther downstream, hoping to find a fishable spot with something trustworthy to stand on, like a firm gravel bar. It wasn't long before I saw an open area ahead. Stepping out of the brush, I could see how the creek cut a broad bend to the right and there was plenty of gravel to walk out on. It was a beautiful morning and I was looking around at the surroundings while I fished the bend using a hook baited with spawn. At some point I noticed that the far bank was steep and curiously "layered." I was intrigued and had to take a closer look.

After reeling my line in, I waded upstream to a place where I could cross without risk of quicksand or over-topping my waders. Moving downstream again along the bank, I saw that the reddish layers were not clay but sand. The red color was from mineral iron in the sand that had oxidized; the clay here is red for the same reason. But how did the sand get way out here and way down beneath all that glacial clay? Looking again at the layers, I thought of how the glacial clay and till rest atop the sandstone all along the coast and throughout the Apostle Islands. Rubbing the sugary sand between my fingers, I realized that the layers were weathered sandstone, not sediments from the glaciers but from another, immensely more distant place and time.

Digging with my fingers in the soil just above the sandstone layers, I found clay, and it was indeed resting upon the sandstone. There is no physical distance between the clay and sandstone, yet in time the distance is more than a billion years. Standing there in waders, with a big fly rod in my hand and the purling water flowing around me, I felt strangely displaced. It was as if I could feel the sweep of time and events swirling endlessly onward around me. I wondered if this was what it was like to be a rock, or to die and be still, to watch the world forever fading into the future. This rock obviously has a good head start on the rest of us.

It was time for shore brunch, today a small bag of peanut M&Ms and a tepid, muddy coffee chaser. After that, there was more fishing. Eventually I caught and released a modest steelhead—modest, that is, for one of these barbarians that sometimes launch themselves across large pools like airborne torpedoes, as if to momentarily defy gravity and the flow of time.

A few days later I was thinking again about the sandstone and the vast gap in time represented by the overlying glacial sediments. In that billion years, life as we know it had arisen from some prototype single cell organism and evolved to the great diversity of life on earth today. Other sediments, or at times lava and other volcanic material, had been deposited on top of this sandstone, only to be eroded away. At some time dinosaurs must have roamed the ceaselessly changing landscapes that had existed here. But there are no fossil dinosaur bones to be found because they were also eroded away. All that remains today of these lost landscapes are questions that may never be completely answered. Those questions are sandwiched right there between the sandstone and glacial clay. We could come here any time we like and lay our hands on them and wonder.

THE STEELHEAD GOD

Here in Chequamegon country spring runoff begins in earnest around the middle of March. By then days of above-freezing temperatures and rain have begun to melt and compact the snow, the icy meltwater trickling off in rivulets to ditches and ephemeral ponds, eventually finding its way to gullies and steep ravines. From there it falls fast, carrying with it the red-brown clay which is everywhere underfoot, tumbling down like so much weak blood into the streams and rivers below.

The valleys themselves remain choked with snow. Ice shelves rim the murky streams and sometimes bridge pools where the current slows. If it has snowed recently, sinewy twists of sooty tag alder lining the banks and midstream boulders will be starkly highlighted in white. If the snow clings to the pines and firs on the hillsides for more than a day or two, a person might be tempted to believe that winter is not yet ready to let go.

But make no mistake about it, winter is waning. Down in the rivers' umber depths the word is out: Spring has arrived. This news is carried all the way to the rivers' mouths where it is broadcast far out into Lake Superior. It is a timeless message that the steelhead have waited for half the winter. And soon, they will heed its calling.

On some appointed Saturday, often the first in April, people begin coming to this country to find out for themselves what the rivers are saying and if the steelhead are listening. But I want to talk about just one river that I know better than the others and about one person who fishes there.

It is the Sioux River, in this season a torrent of cocoa water concealing whatever lies beneath its surface—stumble-boulders, snag limbs, and steelhead. And into this river each spring wades a man who, at first glance, seems rather ordinary. But he is quite extra-ordinary, for he has every square inch of river bottom mapped not just into his memory but into the very fabric of his being. He is a man who probably fishes this river in his dreams as often as he does in waking life. And, waking or dreaming, he fishes it perfectly.

His name is unimportant; you wouldn't recognize it anyhow. I came to regard him as the Steelhead God, which struck me as appropriate long before I learned his real name, for I am convinced this man is a deity of sorts, a reincarnated heron with miraculous powers, able to pluck magnificent fish from these muddy waters at will where mere mortals are destined to fail.

It was opening day of steelhead season some years back when I first encountered the Steelhead God. In the dingy morning light a freezing rain was drizzling from clouds that rubbed their dark underbellies against the treetops. I had arrived early, fully equipped with new waders and fly rod and an assortment of glitzy-looking flies—in short, a greenhorn steelheader. Prepared with what

I took for good advice from well-known national sporting magazines, I thought it would be a simple matter to rollcast a #4 Skykomish Sunrise out into the turbid water and set the hook on an unsuspecting fish.

Long hours later a gnawing suspicion set in that steelheading on the Sioux was somehow different from those Pacific Northwest rivers mentioned in the magazines. There I was, braced against the midstream current, shivering in ice-coated waders, numb fingers turned to unbending hooks, rod guides and fly line clotted with ice. I was a straw in a chocolate milkshake and the icy river was sucking the life out of me through my bloodless legs. Worse, I hadn't had a strike on my fancy flies all morning, much less caught a fish.

At some point I forgot my misery long enough to gaze downstream. Through the rain and mist I could see a dark, brooding figure standing near the next bend—another fisherman holding his long rod level and still, obviously not fly-fishing. When I looked awhile later, the figure hadn't budged an inch. Feeling certain no fish were in my vicinity and never had been, I waded downstream a few dozen yards and resumed fly casting.

Glancing once more downstream, I was shocked to see the mysterious figure's rod bent to the extreme and a silvery steelhead fresh up from the lake tail-dancing across the water. With effortless grace he reached down and in one fluid motion lifted and quickly released the steelhead. Then he stood still as a hunting heron, except for puffs of smoke and the glow of a cigarette from beneath a hood that concealed his face.

This performance, from hook-set to release, he repeated to perfection not ten minutes later in the same place. Then he began moving slowly and with great dignity in my direction, stopping occasionally to hold the tip of his rod over some featureless stretch of water. He passed by without a word, raising and lowering a cigarette to the dark opening in his hood. He was a stout fellow, unremarkably clad: no vest or high-tech neoprene waders and gloves, just a worn green rain poncho draped over patched rubber waders, bare handed, with a huge landing net slung over one shoulder and an old newspaper sack for a creel over the other. The creel looked empty, which seemed odd considering he had just released two fine fish.

He continued upstream until he came to the place where I had stood for several hours, and then began slowly dapping his line. Slack-jawed, I watched as with a flick of his wrist he again set the hook, and the drag on his reel began singing. This time the fish didn't break the surface and it seemed to require of him some effort to haul it in. But eventually the scene played itself out to what I knew would be its inevitable conclusion. It was a magnificent hen steelhead, the kind that people who are into that sort of thing call a wall-hanger. He held it up momentarily to admire it, or perhaps so I could have a better look, before carefully releasing it. Then, either fulfilled or bored with good fishing, he shuffled across the stream, lumbered up the bank and was gone.

Since those first days I've learned about steelheading on the Sioux River. Conventional fly line and steelhead flies, at least early in the season before the water clears, rarely work. Using tougher monofilament and dapping with spawn sacks and Glo Bug yarn flies are a surer bet, with crawlers and various spinners bordering on the exotic but highly effective under the right conditions. These are the baits and lures everyone uses, including the Steelhead God. But merely knowing what to use won't help catch fish if you don't know when and how to use it. This is something the Steelhead God has mastered.

On busy weekend mornings, while scores of other anglers jockey about like so many jittery water bugs, the Steelhead God fishes slowly and with the utmost deliberation. He has the stream wired and knows where steelhead are apt to lie—maybe in a narrow slot in a fast run early in the day, or hiding out in a pocket under a bank after other fishermen have come thrashing through. He works these places harder than a hungry otter, giving the fish plenty of time to reconsider and maybe take his bait after all. And often enough, they do.

One bleak Saturday morning comes to mind as typical of the way the Steelhead God operates. The river had been high, muddy, and frigid—almost gravy and about what you'd expect for this time of year. And, as you might also expect, though there was no shortage of steelheaders, few of them were actually catching any steelhead.

Moving along the bank I came upon an elderly gentleman who was frantically rummaging through his tackle, which was heaped before him. Jumping to his feet and gesturing wildly downstream, he said in a frantic voice, "In the last ten minutes I saw that fella catch four fish—right from a hole I'd already fished in! He's using some kinda big gold spinner, and I don't have a damn one with me!" Neither did I, or anyone else fishing there that morning. That "fella" was the Steelhead God and, as it turns out, he had pulled (and released) nine fish from that hundred-foot stretch of churning water in something like forty-five minutes.

Over the past few seasons I've gotten to know the Steelhead God and discovered he's just one of the locals, a regular guy who drives old beater cars and likes to bring his kids along to fish and cook out in the campground—something few fishermen seem to do these days. But he's also a generous and compassionate fellow, the sort who, if you ask, gladly offers advice and points out places likely to conceal steelhead. His creel is usually empty because he knows better than most that the river and the steelhead can't sustain the increased fishing pressure it's seen lately. He speaks with some authority on these matters because he's fished for steelhead on the Sioux since boyhood, more than forty years now.

I'd never seen him on any other river, but it still came as something of a surprise one day when he told me that now he only fishes the two hundred yards of the Sioux below the Big Rock campground. He does this not by choice, he said, but because of a badly injured back. In fact, his back is so cranky that he can't work and is considered permanently disabled. He said it was his bad back that first got him to slow down on the river, because one false step on the algae-coated rocks could easily result in another trip to the hospital—and a premature, maybe permanent, end to his steelhead fishing.

But if his deliberate way of fishing is born of necessity, it is a necessity he has turned into a virtue. I sometimes wonder how many of us would be capable of doing the same. But then I remember, he *is* the Steelhead God.

A SUPERIOR WILDERNESS

There is nothing like listening to the poetry of loons calling by moonlight to stir the embers of some deeper, almost forgotten question to burning again. This was my discovery one windless, lyrical June evening, as I hunkered alone next to a little campfire on the shores of an island in the "shining big sea water" of Lake Superior. "Home" that night was beneath a tall stand of red and white pines on the sand tombolo that necks between Stockton Island proper and adjacent Presque Isle, in Apostle Islands National Lakeshore.

Presque Isle Bay was flawless, a rare, shining mirror reflecting moon and stars perfectly. The night sky seemed to begin at landfall, sweeping down and away from the beach, then arcing upward again to the zenith. As I banked my little fire and made tea, a small bat spiraled through the flickering yellow light, homing in on a few tiny moths attracted by the glow. Hovering just beyond the fringe of punky camp smoke were uncountable mosquitoes and their electric hum. On a cue known only to them, cherubic chorus frogs began croaking their monotonous love sonnets, which echoed from out the nearby bog. Amid such reflections, attractions, and echoes, it seemed this was a night destined for wakefulness and wonderment.

But sleep was entirely out of the question anyhow. For shortly after moonrise a rising tide of sounds began to wash ashore: vacationing voices yelling and yodeling to guitar sounds, beating bongos, and bellowing tipsy incantations. It was such hoopla as might give the moon second thoughts about further ascent, sufficiently raucous to send the entire amphibian choir diving for the security of the bottom of the bog. The noise was easily traced to its source: a major cocktail party freshly launched on a flotilla of big sailboats rafted together in the bay. The onslaught of this clamor was so sudden, so unexpected, that a bear dropping by for evening tea would hardly have been more surprising. The whole scene seemed misplaced, strangely askew with the serenity and solitude I had experienced only moments before.

Just as foreign was the irritating situation I found myself faced with, having come far to remove myself from the company of my fellow man, seeking tranquillity and wildness. An evening of cacophonous brouhaha wasn't exactly what I had in mind. First inclinations were to douse the fire, grab the tent and pack, and move far elsewhere. Then a more primal notion flashed to my mind: to hurl some projectiles—maybe barbed words—in their direction. But before even less civil acts could be ruminated a gust of night wind came rippling across the bay and whipped a spangle of sparks up from the campfire. This miniature galaxy of twinkling ashes rose through the pines to mingle for a moment with the stars. And before it vanished an awareness was somehow sparked in me that something deeper was at issue here.

On the one hand there was what could be thought of as the epitome of successful modern society, the crème de la crème of this era: dapper, high-spirited, no-bucks-spared people relishing what is as civilized and social a sport as golfing and membership in the local country club. Strictly upper crust. On the other hand, looming on all sides was pure wildness: loons chanting and the vastness of Lake Superior, the big sky above, and the silent, dark, and wild Apostle Islands all around. Perhaps it was the stark incongruity of these two extremes juxtaposed so near one another that finally crystallized the issue for me. With the great purity of wildness found there, I wondered if the Apostle Islands were a true wilderness with all the attendant qualities that go with our conceptions of wilderness, such as remoteness, solitude, and pristine nature. And I wondered if such a wilderness could coexist with sailboaters, kayakers, and hikers.

Eventually the parties fizzled, the deck lights winked out, and a final hoarse yodel faded to insignificance across the expansiveness of the lake. With the solemnity of night regained and the bright lamp of the moon to see by, it seemed there was no better time to wax deep in consideration of these wilderness questions.

For all the wildness believed to be inherent in the northern landscape, it's surprising to realize how very little pristine—capital "W"—Wilderness remains. Nowhere to be found is that wild

country that greeted intrepid French traders Radisson and Groseilliers in the autumn of 1659, when they became the first Europeans
to set foot upon the west shore of a bay the Ojibway inhabitants
called *Shag-a-waum-ik-ong*. The site of their landing is reportedly
somewhere south of Washburn. Anyone happening by there today
and wondering just what Chequamegon Bay and the rest of the
region were like 350 years ago would have to rely heavily on vivid
imagination to supply the missing details. "Wilderness" would of
course come to mind, but only as an abstraction, a word-symbol for
something probably experienced in wilder parts of the continent.
They'd have to squint hard, maybe wait till twilight, and let their
minds create images of wave-cut sandstone cliffs capped with gnarly
white cedars, high-crowned sugar maples and yellow birches, thick
hemlocks and endless tall pines. Moose roamed freely here, as did
wolves, cougars, caribou, and Ojibway people. But such an illusion
lasts only while the eyes remain slitted, only for as long as the
thought can be held onto. A few moments at best. In the parting
there is always the same realization that the old Superior wilderness is gone and can never come back.

Over the years many have tried to conjure up pristine
wilderness in the Northwoods—in all the likely places, including
federally designated wilderness areas. Outside of the Boundary
Waters and the Porcupine Mountains, the magic often fails. Pristine
lands are almost always small groves of trees that were somehow
missed in the days of the Great Cutover. Most of the federal

wildernesses in Wisconsin have been recently clearcut and contain a tangle of old logging roads that, whether someday covered by trees or not, will remain permanent features of these landscapes. Most of these places are also bounded by roads that, because of their small sizes, make it doubly tough to really experience solitude. It also facilitates trespassing by ORVs and snowmobilers, an all too common occurrence.

More recently other forms of degradation have occurred. On a forested hillside just beyond the boundary of the Porcupine Lake Wilderness, someone had the selfish audacity to build a new home that is easily seen from the lake, marring the sense of remoteness and solitude for all who visit there. Handfuls of other reasons exist that everywhere force the same conclusion: Paradise has indeed been lost.

Considering the long and heavy-handed history of resource exploitation in this region, it seems a pipe dream to hope for more than the little bit of wilderness we already have. For today, nearly every acre of forest has been cut at least twice, if not more. And every lake, if not ringed with cottages, has at least some rudimentary sort of public access—maybe just a dirt road leading to a muddy boat launch, but access all the same. Sometimes it's hard to believe that only a few centuries have passed since European habitation of this once-upon-a-time rugged and untamed country began. In that brief interval most every stone seems to have been turned, and most of the "wilderness" tilled, trapped, and chopped out of the land. And it seems the chance to experience genuine wilderness may have been lost as well.

It's not that the inherited landscape isn't beautiful and intriguing, an heirloom of sorts that should be lived with gently and harmoniously, then passed on carefully to forthcoming generations. One lesson of history is that past is past. In fairness we should remember that all the slashing, road building, and ruination of the topsoil wasn't the land's fault. To devalue land, to hold some kind of grudge because it is no longer pristine, would be akin to the same ludicrous logic that holds innocent victims of some calamity responsible for their own bad luck. Probably just as crazy, those who reject their native landscape are in effect severing themselves from it. Thus they cast themselves adrift, squandering their inheritance and foregoing one of the most basic needs of humans, the need to have a sense of our own place within the local landscape. Call it instinctive behavior, the genes of our wild ancestors expressing themselves. Call it whatever you like. But know that it is real, this need to walk the land and realize for ourselves our own vital biological and personal connections with it. Stripped of this sense of place, pristine or not, wildflowers remain forever nameless, forests just so much lumber, and soil something good for standing corn on and burying the dead under.

Be that as it may—despite this tremendous intrinsic worth of the inherited landscape—it still seems somehow unfair that genuine wilderness is so hard to come by. True, small fragments of virgin land can be found tucked away in the folds of the country-side, lost in the leaves of county plat books or held in the public trust as state or privately owned natural areas. But rarer than these precious gems are big tracts of land, cut or uncut, that are more than two miles from the nearest road. And rarest of all are the lands that combine solitude, primal beauty, and ecological integrity—lands that gave definition to the word "wilderness."

To find oneself far from the madding crowds, to be fully steeped in a primitive realm where nature-at-large continues to work unhindered, how deep into the northern countryside must one crawl? Where can a last big hunk of raw, thriving wilderness be found? Despite the cacophonous evening serenade on Presque Isle Bay, or perhaps by way of the grand contrast it afforded, far into the night it slowly dawned on me that I probably had been sitting on the answer to these questions all along: The last of the old Northwest wilder-ness lay before me in the mysterious waters of Chequamegon Bay.

Apostle Islands National Lakeshore, although better known for historic lighthouses and as a mecca for sailboaters, also has to be the biggest and best remaining wilderness in the western Lake Superior region, with 46,000 acres of primitive land spread across twenty-one islands and the mainland. But is it really a wilderness? Those unfamiliar with genuine wilderness and its characteristics might wish to dispute this fact. But people who have experienced wilderness elsewhere, who are keen to note the fine points that separate it from other kinds of land, will unhesitatingly affirm that the Apostle Islands are bona fide wilderness.

Isolation and remoteness go hand in hand within the context of wilderness and, an occasional weekend sailing party in Presque Isle Bay notwithstanding, the Apostle Islands are amply endowed with both. This is true mainly by virtue of the fact that they are islands, and just getting out to them is cumbersome at best—impossible at worst. The Lakeshore is a surprisingly big place, spread over 250 square miles. Outer Island, the most distant of the Apostles, is twenty miles from the usual departure site of Bayfield and accessible only in favorable weather. The most obvious impairment to gaining any island, even any of the inner islands, is that a boat is required. But not any bucket will do. Instead, the preferred vessel should be seaworthy enough to endure most anything that Lake Superior's infamously capricious weather can throw at it. Or at least fast enough to get to a safe harbor in a hurry. Still, even the best boat will be of no use if not equipped with a skipper who has enough savvy to navigate safely the wily, frigid waters. Only the foolhardy take lightly the old, ominous adage, "Lake Superior never gives up her dead." Sudden weather swings can turn placid seas into wicked six- or eight-foot breaking swells in only minutes. In a gale fifteen- to twenty-five-foot waves are not uncommon. Superior's historically long list of shipwrecks and drownings is testimonial enough to the wildness of its waters.

Lacking a boat, nautical familiarity with Lake Superior, or both, the usual methods of travel to the islands are either by water taxi, which can be prohibitively expensive, or the concession boat tour, which stops briefly at Stockton, Manitou, and Raspberry Islands. Sea kayaking is also gaining in popularity, and is probably the best means of approaching the Apostles on their own terms. But again, to safely paddle these waters requires more than just a sea kayak; paddlers must be experienced and familiar with the unique conditions found on the largest body of fresh water in the world. It's worth mentioning that for much of the season a wet suit isn't usually considered optional equipment for Lake Superior kayakers —it's essential gear that could be lifesaving.

Going ashore on an island can also prove challenging or even daunting, depending on one's inclinations. The islands' dense forest understory and boggy terrain make for interesting, albeit difficult cross-country travel. The only really sane way to move about is by trail, which most islands have in some form or other. And yet even on a trail, what may well be the single greatest barrier to humans' use of the islands remains to be encountered. For besides beaver ponds and bogs, the forest floor is pockmarked with countless wet depressions, and "therein lies the rub." These are the breeding grounds of what must amount to googols of mosquitoes and biting flies. In the Upper Great Lakes, bugs are as likely to keep the timid and thin-skinned out of the woods as grizzly bears are in the West.

Because of these combined hindrances to travel, just a few popular sandspits and lighthouses see anywhere near the kind of concentrated use that the developed Stockton Island tombolo receives. And nearly all of this use comes between June and September, much of it on weekends. Thus the islands' inaccessibility and rugged nature, the fickle weather, the dense forests and bugs— in short, all the exigencies of a wilderness condition—render most of the Apostle Islands a sanctuary for solitude.

As elsewhere in the Great Lakes, neither did the Apostle Islands' forests escape the bite of the axe during the logging era. In fact, much of the area's history is closely tied to logging and the development of sawmills on Chequamegon Bay. But there is an important difference between logging history here and that of the famous Pineries on the mainland. For while logging commenced in the Apostles at an earlier date, about 1830, over the years it proceeded at a much less feverish pace. While Lullabye Camp (a small logging outfit) continued to operate on Outer Island until the early 1960s, some of the islands haven't been logged in a century or more, and then were only selectively cut for pine, or for hemlock whose bark was collected and sent to tanneries where it was used in the tanning process.

Neither did this low-impact kind of logging claim all of the islands' forests. Five of the twenty-one islands within the Lakeshore were not logged and remain in their primal condition to this day. These virgin forests are astonishingly pristine and beautiful;

nothing comparable in size and quality can be found elsewhere in Wisconsin—no other place even comes close. Several of the other islands also possess large stands of virgin timber. These rare, intact forests of massive old hemlocks, white pines, and yellow birches never felt the sting of saw steel; their understories remain a dense tangle of rare American yew because white-tailed deer never existed on them or were once present only in low numbers. And so while some of the Apostle Islands' forests aren't much farther ahead in recovering from the effects of cut-and-run logging than their mainland counterparts, the majority are either pristine or well on their way to returning to an old growth condition. It's worth noting that even the better known wilderness park across the lake, Isle Royale National Park, cannot boast of so much pristine forest. Neither can any other national park in the Upper Midwest.

Because the islands' forests were either disturbed long ago or not at all, it would be expected that their flora and fauna are both thriving and diverse. And so they are. Black bear, fisher, red fox, and otter all roam free. No less than six eagle nests were found in the islands last year, and rare falcons known as taiga merlins have been sighted regularly, and an active nest was found. The endangered piping plover, which historically nested in the Apostles, has once again been sighted on sandy stretches of beach, and may eventually renest here. The rare great gray owl has been found nesting in remote areas, as have red-winged crossbills and Wilson's warblers. During migration the islands' forests and beaches become important resting and feeding sites for almost two hundred species of birds, including large numbers of warblers and shorebirds.

Wildflowers are also profligate in the Apostle Islands. Pink lady's slippers and the elsewhere uncommon dragon's mouth orchid bloom abundantly in Lakeshore forests and bogs, and over a dozen other orchids are found here. Many rare plant species recognized on Wisconsin's official list of threatened and endangered species also inhabit the islands, including butterwort, lenticular sedge, and arctic primrose. Through the growing season something blooming and wonderful is found at every turn.

Wilderness is also often associated with scenery that inspires a sense of grandeur and awe. In the Apostle Islands, even the usual low-angle views available from a boat are sublime. Red sandstone cliffs and clay bluffs rim large verdant islands that sweep across the horizon between the vastnesses of lake and sky. Nearer at hand are dramatic, wave-cut ledges and caves—fog shrouded on cool autumn mornings, sun baked in summer, or glazed with rime ice and festooned with giant icicles in winter. Islands are crowned with big trees that in exposed places are sometimes gnarled and wind tattered. And there are the sandspits, tombolos, and cuspate forelands, with their narrow sandy beaches crested with beach grass, Canada wild rye, beach pea, and other maritime grasses and flowers. From shore or on the lake vast views can be had that try the resolving power of even the sharpest eyes. To the south the ancient Penokee and Gogebic Ranges bulge over the horizon. To the east the outline of the Porcupine Mountains reveals the origin of the name given them by the Ojibway. And forty miles to the north the high escarpment of Lake Superior's north shore looms like the Great Wall of China, a dark declivity that drops from view to the northeast beyond the earth's curvature. Such views help us to grasp the vastness of the world and perhaps to reflect with humility on the significance of our own small place in it.

There are countless other qualities found in the Apostle Islands that distinguish them as wilderness and increase their importance for people beyond inspiring scenery. But these virtues are the sort that are hard to define in concrete terms. The great naturalist and outdoorsman Sigurd Olson referred to them as "intangibles." For instance, how do you explain what changes inside you when you lay a hand on a billion-year-old slab of sandstone and feel the sweep of all those years? When you see a chickadee and realize it is looking back at you, how do you describe the silent exchange of awareness that takes place? Far from anywhere, alone in a stand of big hemlocks, what is it that makes you want to stay there? When the pines sing in the wind and big rollers come crashing ashore on a remote beach, could you really say just what it is that you feel at that moment? Experiences, feelings, and encounters at the edge of description, yet all real and meaningful—in short, "intangibles." But there is no need to explain intangibles. I think that in a very deep way they bring us back in touch with the world. And when we leave the wilderness, we carry those feelings and ineffable perceptions with us. Intangibles remain among the greatest gifts of wilderness, including the Apostle Islands wilderness.

Wilderness also presents the opportunity to experience first-hand mankind's aeons-old relationship with wildness, to live and move about in a wild state. Out of such experiences can grow a more tangible understanding of how wilderness has shaped our human spirit, and in particular the American mind. It is easy to forget that humans evolved to our present-day form over trackless ages in wilderness, and that until very recently it was our home. Evolutionarily speaking, it has been only a matter of days since we stepped forth from the woods. A mere fifty centuries of "civilized" life can barely be expected to have changed the wild blood that still rushes through our veins. And neither can it be expected to have altered the strong physical, psychological, and spiritual bonds we have with wild things and wild places. Recently espoused notions that people now live outside of nature, that nature has somehow ended, and that technology negates the need to maintain our relationship with wilderness amount to mere technocratic propaganda. Wilderness is as much a part of what we are today as it ever was. In light of the vast environmental carnage that is taking place throughout the world, wilderness is of greater importance to us now than ever before.

Wilderness may have been the raw stuff out of which our forefathers carved our nation, but in turn it did much to uniquely sculpt us as a people. This birthplace of the "American mind" was a great wilderness called "the frontier," and for over four hundred years the supply was seemingly limitless. When the land was still big and men yet knew they were small, few thought of a time when the frontier would be gone. But as the Wisconsin-born historian Frederick Jackson Turner documented, the frontier era ended by 1890, and vanished with it was much of the wilderness of the conterminous states and territories. There would never again be unknown country to the west, where life could begin anew. No more the wilderness that cultivated our uniquely American sense of self-reliance. Gone forever the unbounded forests and plains where we learned to cherish our individual freedom. Never again would Americans wake each day to the promise of a young and bountiful land, the source of a genuine national optimism that has waned in more recent times.

Strangely enough, after centuries of turmoil and struggle settling the land, no sooner had the frontier closed than people began to realize what a tragic loss this meant for the nation. And it was with this recognition that a national movement was begun to preserve the fragments of wilderness left in the wake of settlement. A hundred years later, thanks to the efforts of several generations of wilderness defenders, sanctuaries of wilderness remain as an enduring resource. Wilderness offers something of deeper, more lasting value to future generations, benefits that can be found nowhere else. As the famous wilderness advocate Bob Marshall put it, only in wilderness can the "precious value of the timeless, the mysterious, and the primordial" be preserved in a world that is otherwise "overrun by split-second schedules, physical certainty, and man-made superficiality." And to know such a wilderness, said wilderness defender Howard Zahniser, "is to know a profound humility, to recognize one's littleness, to sense dependence and interdependence, indebtedness and responsibility." By experiencing wilderness we become more whole, more fully human, and develop a deeper appreciation for all life. "In wildness," Henry David Thoreau's oft-quoted aphorism offers, "is the preservation of the world." Over the years the truth of these words endures, reverberating anew in each generation like the gentle song of a hermit thrush, the last voice heard in the woods each night, the first one heard each morning. It is a song we can all abide by.

Given the Apostle Islands' remoteness and size, the pristine nature of many of the islands, the abundant qualities of wilderness everywhere present, and the enduring legacy that it could bestow upon present and future generations, it is time to ask: Are the Apostle Islands within the Apostle Islands National Lakeshore not a genuine wilderness, wild as any other in the eastern United States and deserving of official congressional designation as a federal wilderness?

Apparently others are reaching this important conclusion, as evidenced by the General Management Plan for Lakeshore. The plan proposes a study of more than 40,000 acres, or 97 percent, of the land area of the Apostle Islands. As required by the Wilderness Act of 1964, a wilderness study has to be done on all wild lands under federal management to determine their suitability for official designation as wilderness. Once the study is completed and recommendations are made, Congress will debate the findings and, if a bill can be successfully drafted and passed, the area will be officially designated and become part of the National Wilderness System.

Because it would be difficult to dispute the wilderness character of the Apostle Islands, and because official designation would do little to change the way the area is used, the issue isn't likely to be controversial. Official designation may be some years off, however, because of budget cutbacks and the National Lakeshore's priority on its operations, visitor services, and maintenance. Wilderness designation is a very expensive process, and without additional funding from the National Park Service or a special allocation from Congress, official wilderness designation may be many years away. However, public support in the form of letters and phone calls from concerned citizens and organizations to congressmen, senators, and Park Service officials may play an important role in seeing that money is allocated to get the study underway and the essential recommendations passed on to Congress.

In the meantime, it's comforting to know that at least one last big piece of wilderness exists in Wisconsin after all. It's out there in Lake Superior—the silent craggy cliffs, the tall dark forests, the cold deep waters. And it waits for no official designations, for no one special. It never has and it never will. The Apostle Islands wilderness is just out there, letting the centuries wash against its shores. Official designation, after all, is really done for the good of people, recognizing and preserving as it does our birthright as Americans to the wilderness, and providing a sanctuary where we can experience our enduring and essential relationship with things wild and free.

BOG WALKING
IN BIRD TIME

Ten thousand birds sing in the sunrise.
Ten thousand years revolve without change.
All this will never be again.

KENNETH REXROTH,
The Wheel Revolves

The sun had just risen above the pines and maples on a fine, cool June morning. It warmed me where I stood, slightly confused, a vague feeling of uncertainty having followed me down the long beach like a nagging sandfly. Something about this place was different from my last visit a year ago. But what?

Before me was a wildly tangled thicket of perfume-scented sweet gale and sooty speckled alder that screened the view beyond. Behind me, a narrow dune sparsely covered with beach pea, beach grass, Canada wild rye, and wormwood gave way to just a sliver of sand beach—the very tenuous edge of terra firma and the restless fresh waters of that vast inland sea called Lake Superior. This remote beach and dune are part of a quarter-mile-long barrier spit at the

mouth of the Sand River, which is on the mainland and within the protective legal boundary of Apostle Islands National Lakeshore.

The first reason for my presence there was business; I was working as an "atlaser" for the Wisconsin Breeding Bird Atlas project. It was my job to determine, as best I could, which species of birds were present and to gather as much evidence as possible to verify if alder flycatchers, for instance, were nesting in the natural wetland created by the barrier spit and the backwaters of the Sand River. The spit and wetland exist where and as they do by virtue of a natural compromise. The river supplies the sand and, depending on lake level in any given year, the waves and currents either help build and shape the spit or carry it away.

Backtracking to the beach, I crouched down where small, cold waves pushed by a light northwest wind lapped over my old running shoes, which work well in those marshy or boggy places where one's feet, or possibly much more, will invariably get soaked. Looking closely, I could see sand grains being lifted and carried ahead an inch or so with each incoming wave, only to be pulled back again as the wave receded. This action, and the way the waves were angling ashore from the northwest, seemed to be ever so subtly zig-zagging the entire beach, grain by grain, eastward. Looking back in the direction I had come from, I could see what it was that had changed.

The year before, I recalled, the beach had been much broader and more richly covered with grasses. But this year the lake's surface was much higher, perhaps six inches or more above last year's level. Higher water and persistent wave action together could explain the serious beach erosion that had occurred. But then I began to imagine the bulldozer-like effects of autumn's northeasters and northwesters: blowing hard for days, the storm surges raise water levels near shore, and the massive rolling breakers expend their tremendous energies as they crash ashore, dumping uncountable tons of water upon beaches, spits, clay banks, and rock ledges all along the coast. The fury of such great storms could devour and carry away much of a small beach, such as this one, in a night.

Attempts to better regulate the unpredictable variations of Lake Superior's surface level at the lock and dam works at Sault Ste. Marie, Ontario, have been an ongoing frustration for some government officials. It has also been a source of encouragement for many others who inhabit the shore around the lake. The exposed roots of beach plums, sand cherries, and the grasses, the small lakeside leaning pines and birches all tell a truer story: despite seemingly chaotic changes in lake levels and the apparent building or severe cutting away of the spit in a given year, over the long haul there has evolved a natural stability based on continuous change.

Was Heraclitus, who first propounded, "All is flow, nothing is the same," standing on a sandspit along the Grecian coast when that idea came upon him? It is more than a little heartening to realize that, despite centuries of amassed knowledge and technologies, despite lines drawn on maps and laws harangued in the body politic, there are yet places on the earth beyond complete dominion and control by humans. The Big Lake is one such place, and it is a kind of great good fortune, a blessing if you will, that is only of late becoming more fully and widely recognized.

Returning to the brush, I carefully wound my way through the tangled stems and branches. It was an unexpected workout of a kind not yet available in gymnasiums and health spas. Sweating profusely and ushered forward by eager mosquitoes and biting gnats, I soon was out of the brush and hip-deep in leatherleaf, bog laurel, and bog rosemary.

Looking back, I could see that the wall of brush I had thrashed through formed the outer edge, or "moat," of the bog. The stability of the dry sand had given way to the quakiness of a floating sphagnum mat, which seemed wetter and "quakier" than I could recall. The bog level is also affected by lake level, not only over long time scales but on much smaller, daily and hourly scales because of seiches. A *seiche* is a short-term rise or fall in lake level. Seiches are sometimes caused by strong winds but more typically by large differences in air pressure between one part of the lake and another. If there is low pressure over the Sand River bog and strong onshore winds, the level of the bog could rise dramatically. If there is high pressure and offshore winds, the level in the bog could fall; boats are occasionally stranded in coastal wetlands for hours because of such seiches.

Moving ahead and paying attention again to the birds, I soon heard a male marsh wren singing, then saw him flash off after another male wren who had horned in on his territory—a quasi-definable boundary of heaths and space known only to the wrens.

Standing quietly, trying to listen carefully beyond the insect drone, I could hear the songs of other birds coming from every direction. Nearby, a few male yellow warblers were vehemently singing their spirited ode to love, "sweet-sweet-sweeter-than-sweet," and I watched a female with a small dragonfly clenched in her bill disappear into the sedges and leatherleaf, doubtless to feed the youngsters in her nest. As if in a contest, which in a deeper sense they were, Nashville warblers took turns loudly singing their songs in a stand of tamarack farther across the bog. From the branches of willows and pines along the spit, darting American redstarts flashed bold orange patches on their wings and tails, fervently singing their unique version of that one timeless song of life sustaining life.

The air over the bog was dense with the revelry of birds. The fervor of their songs, the small, intricate energies of their lives being played out at this place-in-time, brought questions to mind. How many years, or millennia, have Nashville warblers been migrating north to breed in this coastal bog? How far back in time was it when a redstart first became a redstart? And more frightening, how much longer will migratory songbirds, like these warblers, continue to exist with the ongoing devastation of their rainforest wintering grounds in Central and South America?

There is relatively little fossil evidence of the more recently evolved birds, like warblers and vireos, and their times and places of origin are objects of much speculation. The familial relationships of modern birds, however, have been more or less worked out. This was done by the time-honored method of comparing anatomical features and, more recently, genetic material. But even here reinterpretations are not usual. And so it is known that, for instance, a Nashville warbler is more closely related to a blue-winged warbler than it is to a redstart. But no one knows with certitude the time and place of origin of redstarts. In terms of human life we can merely say that they have been here a long time.

Ironically, biologists today are better able to see the future of these birds taking shape than they are to understand their evolutionary origins. Through breeding bird censuses, migratory bird counts, and atlas projects like the one I was working on, ornithologists have discovered large declines in migratory bird populations throughout the United States over the past twenty years. The loss of rainforests is at the heart of the matter. Yet even here in Wisconsin, researchers linked the breaking up of large forest tracts to major losses in breeding songbird populations. Recently, another study found that Wisconsin has millions of feral cats, which are responsible for the deaths of untold millions of songbirds every year. Without preserving enough tropical rainforests and the integrity of their breeding grounds here in the North, the future of many of these birds looks bleak.

Walking farther, I noticed a large garter snake sunning itself atop a mound of sphagnum. It was rather round for a snake, quite well fed it seemed, and I wondered what sort of food supply might help a snake grow so large. Here and there in the sphagnum around the snake, insectivorous pitcher plants were in full bloom, the alluring reddish petals of their nodding flowers suspended on a stalk above the large tubular leaf in which they trap and "digest" insects. Beside these were little yellow sundews, with their tiny leaves lined with sticky hairs to attract and snare unsuspecting flies. Like pitcher plants, they also secrete enzymes to digest their prey. Had this snake grown fat by robbing the sundew or pitcher plants of their entrapped bugs? The thought was intriguing, but there were plenty of other creatures for a big snake to feed upon, like bog lemmings, shrews, tree frogs or green frogs, or the larvae of many kinds of insects.

Like most plant life, sundew and pitcher plants require a significant amount of nitrogen to grow and reproduce. Bogs by their nature are nitrogen poor, but these insectivorous plants evolved from ancestoral plants over the great reaches of time to get some of their nitrogen from insects and coexist perfectly in a sphagnum bog. They exist nowhere else. To have found a sundew or pitcher plant is to have found a bog. And to have discovered a bog is to have chanced upon an unbroken puzzle where all the pieces fit together perfectly.

Moving east along the edge of the tamaracks, I heard several Connecticut warblers and then saw a male moving about in the lower branches of one tree. Before long, I saw other flowers out in the open sphagnum, and I veered away to see what they were. En route I passed a beautiful clump of wild iris, their fresh, perfectly formed, bright blue petals the obvious reason for their other common name, blue flag. Stepping through a wetter pocket of the bog, I found the pretty white flowers of several wild calla, which are closely related to skunk cabbage and jack-in the-pulpits. This family of plants is also insectivorous, attracting flies and other insects that feed on carrion by releasing a fetid odor. Then, a few yards away, I found the flowers that had lured me so often from my work.

Dozens of bog buckbean—an odd name for such a pretty white gentian—were blooming before me. With the inside of their flower petals frilled with long white hairs, their beauty has always seemed exotic to me because they resemble no other flower that I have seen. Their presence adds yet another layer of richness to the life of this place. It speaks of a kind of unbroken integrity that has endured for thousands of years. Scattered around the buckbean were the delicate white blossoms of three-leaved false Solomon's seal, which is closely related to several kinds of false Solomon's seal found on drier ground. In a shallow pocket of water I found yet another insectivorous plant, the common bladderwort, which has tiny, submerged bladders that capture and digest small aquatic insects and larvae.

Standing once again, just looking around, I saw a few pinkish blossoms nestled among the deep greens of the bog. These were flowers I had seen on my first visit to this bog years ago. They are aptly named dragon's mouth orchids for the shape of their single, brilliant pink flower. But name aside, I am not sure I have ever seen a flower more beautiful. Kneeling down beside one of them in the sphagnum, I felt as happy as I did the first time I saw them. Like the buckbean, at first their form and beauty, which we are unaccustomed to, seem outlandish. And yet, it seems perfectly at home among the sphagnum, sedges, and cranberries. And it is.

Before crossing the moat and returning to the sandspit to hike out to the truck, I turned around for a long last look at the bog, to try to take it all in, somehow bring it home. I recalled Henry David Thoreau's desire "to live deep and suck out all the marrow of life." There was no need to bring anything home. Like so many other wonderful places, the Sand River bog would continue to endure. I realized that I could return any time to suck out the marrow—the wonders, the mysteries, the beauty—of life. And so I have.

FINE TUNING

To seek is as important as to find.

WENDELL BERRY

In late June I heard a rumor that rarity existed nearby. I heard that back in the seventies a small cluster of rare orchids called auricled twayblades had been found somewhere in the area of the Sioux River. Auricled twayblades are part of a "boreal pattern" of rare plants scattered throughout northeastern North America: a group of living relics left behind as other cold-loving plants shifted north in the wake of retreating glaciers 8,000 years ago.

Common is one word that has *never* been used to describe twayblades. Like float copper and wolves, you find them where you find them. The Sioux River twayblades, I was told, had been found only once since then, in the early eighties by the famous orchidologist Frederick Case.

When I first heard this story I didn't think much of it. But a few days later, when I found myself digging through a stack of musty, arcane botany books in the basement of the Dexter Library in Ashland, I realized I had been bitten by the gnat of intrigue.

Auricled twayblades, I read, belong to the genus *Listera*, so named in honor of Martin Lister, a flower-loving seventeenth century English naturalist. Described as "more curious than beautiful," twayblades are primitive as orchids go; their pollinia, or pollen masses, are powdery and they have only one fertile stamen. More recently evolved orchids have sticky pollinia and two or three fertile stamen.

Details like these may seem inane, yet upon such minutiae first hinged the modern theories of evolution. For it was Charles Darwin's discovery of these special adaptations of orchid flowers, which insures cross-pollination, that confirmed his theory of evolution, this based on his study of several kinds of orchids, including *Listera*. In a letter to the eminent botanist Sir Joseph Hooker in 1861, Darwin wrote, "I never was more interested in any subject in my life than this of Orchids." Small wonder.

Still preoccupied with twayblades a week later, on a steamy-hot evening I finally drove north from town to the Sioux River. The thought looping through my brain at the time was that, besides the Sioux population, the only other records of auricled twayblades occurring in Wisconsin dated from the thirties. These had been found on the west side of the Bayfield Peninsula near Cornucopia, and on the east side near Barksdale on Chequamegon Bay. Yet Professor Case has said that, because auricled twayblades are such small and otherwise unremarkable-looking plants, they are "probably much more frequent and overlooked along the larger rivers in the vicinity of Lake Superior," and that "careful searching may reveal their presence." His words became a kind of mantra that helped crowd doubts of finding them from my mind; I was convinced I was going to *find* these twayblades.

After easing down a small hill and rounding a bend, the highway runs directly across the Sioux River's flood plain. Here the river runs in wide channels, which meander through a broad marsh before joining a slough near its mouth. The mouth opens into the northwest side of Lake Superior's Chequamegon Bay. In midsummer this marsh is verdant with cattails, sedges, and bulrushes, and it is brightened by flowers of lake cinquefoil and blue flag. From across the marsh drift timeless voices of redwinged blackbirds and common yellowthroats, marsh wrens, and black ducks. Large speckled alders crowd the riverbanks and are scattered elsewhere about the marsh.

Not far upstream the river flows out of a swamp forest of black ash, red maple, white cedar, and tag alder. Dead, barkless hulks of American elms still stand among the other trees there; pileated woodpeckers have battered away at these snags for years.

Abrupt, tree-covered clay bluffs—lakebed sediments laid down about 10,000 years ago when Glacial Lake Duluth's surface was hundreds of feet higher than Lake Superior's present level— jut up from the edge of the flood plain. Once covered with giant red and white pines, the forests on these slopes were logged in the late 1800s and have regrown to mature red oak, paper birch, smaller white and red pines, and balsam fir.

Miles upstream the Sioux itself runs hard over Precambrian sandstone country rock, scouring away the glassy quartz grains as it cuts its way down to lake level. When the river floods its banks, which is not often, this sand is laid down on the flood plain; the rest of the time it slowly saltates along the bottom, pushed by the current until it is finally washed out into the lake. There currents and waves rework the clean sand to form the two-mile-long Bayview Beach.

According to Professor Case, it is this raw alluvial sand, deposited beneath alders during irregular periods of flooding, that provides the right growing conditions for auricled twayblades. Less commonly, they have also been found on several Lake Superior islands beneath alders in the sandy swales on the backsides of beaches.

The highway crosses both channels of the Sioux; the first bridge spans the main channel and the second the north channel, or slough. Easing off the road I parked the car on the shoulder close to the main channel. Cliff swallows, which were nesting beneath the concrete bridge, swooped and twirled above its deck, oblivious to me and to the cars speeding by. From the river's edge a spotted sandpiper doddering in the grass regarded me suspiciously as I closed the car door and unceremoniously climbed into a knot of alders. Such a sudden immersion caught me by surprise; it was like belly-flopping into water that was unexpectedly cold and murky. It was visually jarring beneath the alders: a dimly lit chlorophyll sky, with vision reduced to chaotic tangles of sooty speckled limbs and saw-toothed leaves. And nothing else.

Under these conditions attenuation comes naturally enough. Unable to see far, I could only focus on what was near at hand. Bent at the waist like a cartoon sleuth, I ponderously examined the ground beneath every alder clump for evidence of twayblades, high-stepping and wriggling along the bank in the direction of the confluence with the slough. Sweat dripped from my nose, chin, and elbows, and the mosquitoes did what they always do.

Eventually I found the slough and followed its bank back toward the highway. Conditions beneath the alders appeared ideal, but I had not found the twayblades. Enthusiasm flickered and waned, but I continued anyhow, buoyed up by the prolonged state of concentration that had overtaken me. And besides, I still had to make my way back to the car. As the search continued no alder clump went unnoticed; each was fully inspected: *No, not beneath this one either.*

Compelled to find something, *anything*, to save the day, I began to compile a list of what I saw: sedges, sedges, and more sedges; plucked feathers from what had been a common yel-lowthroat; shells of snails and clams; some weathered beer cans; the faded plastron of a very small painted turtle; a few Canada mayflowers gone to seed. The mayflowers were about the same size and shape as twayblades, and on finding them I felt sudden pangs of excitement until I recognized them as impostors.

Two hours of intense, fruitless searching brought me stumbling up onto the warm pavement of the highway. Wet feet, ripped pants, and a rash of insect bites were my souvenirs. The sun had set, the swallows gone to roost, the traffic all but disappeared. Ambling back to where I'd parked the car, I noticed the banks west of the first bridge were lined with alders as far as I could see up the river. This unexplored ground looked promising and I wondered if I had wasted my time searching the wrong place. It was a hope, something to take home and sleep on. Somehow it was easier to walk away empty-handed knowing unturned stones remained.

For living things, at least, rarity is the next-to-last result of an unsuitable arrangement with the world. Extinction is the final result. Be it wallflowers, whippoorwills, or walleyes, life is most successful at the business of living—of survival and reproduction—where its peculiar requirements are best fulfilled. Where these essentials are wholly lacking, existence is untenable.

But don't be fooled. However plausible or reasonable the foregoing explanation may be, it is too conveniently simple to be useful in understanding that frail and tentative realm of existence just this side of what Taoists sometimes refer to as "the void." Like bungee jumpers and flame swallowers, rare things are idiosyncratic, with their own unique and highly precise set of conditions needed for continued existence. Because these conditions are met only under the most special of circumstances, rare things tend to be few and far between; flame swallowers, to my knowledge, have never been common.

Many of the threats rare organisms face stem from problems inherent to all small populations, not the least of which is inbreeding, which causes a loss in the variability of inherited traits, some of which may be critical to the species' survival. If the only traits left in a small population of bungee jumpers were weak ankles and vertigo, odds are they wouldn't survive for long. Another problem small populations face is the disastrous effects of seemingly insignificant chance events; an old tree limb falling in just the wrong place can wreak havoc on the last of anything.

In trying to understand the nature of rareness, biologists since Darwin's time have incorporated what they know about the attributes of rare plants and animals into burgeoning theories and mathematical models about speciation, population dynamics, diversity, island biogeography, to name a few. The resulting answers, the answers to the questions of rarity, have been anything but simple. Frequently they have only led to more questions or speculations, or pointed to a need for further research.

Why people search for rarities may be as difficult to answer as the question of what makes a flower, frog, beetle, or lichen rare. For what is it that pulls at the heels and compels otherwise rational people to abandon prosperous endeavors in search of something not likely to be found? Quests to high mountains for answers to the meaning of life seem more reasonable. Why should anyone suffer long hours in boggy, bug-infested alder bottoms on the outside chance they might run across a nondescript little green plant called the auricled twayblade?

The most obvious answer is because it's the right thing to do: what is not found cannot be saved, and what is unknown can easily be destroyed. This is, after all, the age of environmental enlightenment, of greater awareness and sensitivity toward the multitude of other consciousnesses living in the world beside us. "Saving the pieces" is no longer looked upon as just a nice thing to do: it has become an ethical duty. From Aldo Leopold's *Sand County Almanac* to Wendell Berry's *The Unsettling of America* to Gary Snyder's *The Practice of the Wild*, the fact seems well cemented that we are each of us stewards of the earth and have moral obligations to protect the integrity of its living systems, including the lands we happen to live upon and depend upon daily. And part of this duty to the land includes finding and protecting rare things.

But there may be other reasons besides moral obligation to seek rarities. What about play? Leopold said that whatever is done in the name of play requires no justification. His logic is unassailable, but it doesn't really elucidate just what it is, what sort of enjoyment or satisfaction, people get out of searching for rarities. Wendell Berry hints at it this way: "The thing is to be attentively present.

What is to be found, or not found, is always there. The only condition is your being there and being watchful."

Like that familiar and timeless game of children, seeking what is hidden or unknown is a kind of play that is basic to our very nature. To play the game well, being attentively present is really "the thing." Seeking merely to find is an inferior kind of play. Fully attentive play reveals more than what was sought, leads to a deeper realization, a fuller satisfaction: that of finding one's place, wherever that may be, in the world. Seeking, touching, tasting, hearing, probing, wandering far, and dallying near are some of the ways we have of being attentive. They are our means of fully inhabiting the lands we live upon, and the personal landscapes within each of us.

Rarity seems to be a flighty concept. It is a small white bird winging through a snowstorm. Luck is catching a glimpse of this fleeting bird. Wisdom is learning to see the snowflakes that were always there. In our searchings we may emerge from the woods or the marsh empty-handed, but our eyes will have been opened.

I returned to the Sioux River a few days later. After parking the car, I sat on the bridge abutment awhile thinking about how I should proceed and how I might improve my chances of finding these auricled twayblades. That's when the idea of fine tuning came to mind.

Fine tuning can be thought of as that fundamental re-adjustment of perception that takes place in the minds of those who would search for slivers of rarity among haystacks of the common. Like hunters of old, seekers of rarity learn to unhinge their minds, to let thoughts of elsewhere and else-wise dissipate while their senses attenuate. Forgotten gifts return. Ears prick at a distant vireo's song and a cicada's buzz, at pine limbs creaking in wind and stones clacking in streams: all familiar. Eyes dart and scan, recomposing the puzzle, moving swiftly like hunting foxes through field and wood. Molecule by molecule the nose sifts the air for subtler clues: bear musk, a hint of ripe blackberries, whiffs of distant smoke. Arms and legs swing and flex easily, move in inherited rhythms of readiness to stop, stoop, examine—or fleet away in a new direction.

Time as an abstraction founders, while a sense of present real world time takes hold. To hurry or rest is pointless; there is only this looking, only this eternal Now. The focus of consciousness becomes that of complete attentiveness to every detail and to nothing in particular. This is the art of fine tuning, of slipping into a state of mind others have sometimes referred to as "the naturalist's trance."

But recognition requires something more than this trance-like state. Some kind of familiarity with the place, with what is common and what is not, seems essential. Known and expected images and patterns are held up against a light in the back of the mind; against what is familiar, the rare and unusual contrast starkly: *This* is different.

Fine tuning is what I was thinking about as I stepped off the highway shoulder and stooped to follow a fishermen's path through a difficult maze of large, old speckled alders. At a point perhaps two hundred yards from the highway, I was down on hands and knees crawling through alders when right under my nose there appeared several small plants that looked strangely familiar. They were roughly six inches tall with just a single pair of tiny heart-shaped leaves opposite each other midway up their stems. Above the leaves was a very small, open cluster of pale greenish flowers already going to seed. Suddenly I felt giddy and laughed out loud as a wave of realization swept over me: *These were auricled twayblades!*

I lay down on my belly to look closer; what I needed to verify was the tell-tale split in the lower "lip" of the flowers. Only one flower was in sufficiently good condition to show its elongated, flat "lip" with a cleft at the end that was about a quarter of the lip's total length. That was the clincher, the defining characteristic, the proof that something truly rare was here.

Then for a minute, the wind slowly went out of my sails. My mission seemed over. I felt sure these twayblades were the same ones found back in the seventies. Then I recalled Case's quote: "... probably being much more common along major rivers along the south shore of Lake Superior than previously realized." It was still early in the evening, so I decided to continue looking for tway-blades on the outside chance of finding more. Thirty feet away I found another small cluster tucked beneath a huge old alder, just a few feet from the river.

Feeling very lucky, I backtracked through the alders hoping to find other twayblades that could easily have been missed the first time through. In waning light I crawled out of the alders. From the bridge I watched a small caddisfly hatch and listened to white-throated sparrows singing their last songs of the day.

Driving home that night, I wondered just how uncommon or common twayblades might actually turn out to be on the Bay-field Peninsula and where else they might exist. If on the banks of the Sioux, then why not the Onion or the Siskiwit rivers? Why not indeed! In the back of my mind I began to lay plans to resume my search for rarity when the auricled twayblades flower ever so briefly again next June.

BLUEBERRY ROADS

On the Bayfield Peninsula, gravel, mud, and sand roads are the rule rather than the exception. For every mile of asphalt roadway here there exist at least fifty more or less passable miles of terrain-hugging, unpaved country road of widely varying construction and quality. In light of this revelation, it should come as no surprise to learn that there isn't a traffic light in all of Bayfield County; we simply have no need for one. Just as "all roads lead to Rome," if followed far enough, many of our country roads eventually meander into an unpopulated hinterland known locally as the barrens.

Some years ago I discovered this fact myself, for many of my unplanned Saturday excursions somehow wound up in the barrens, where I found myself slowly motoring along its rutted sandy lanes. I emphasize *slowly*, because driving fast on these quasi-roads can be perilous business, and the slow deliberation required to negotiate them can be a good tonic for heebie-jeebies brought on by the sort of fast living so prevalent in late twentieth century life.

On these half-wild thoroughfares it's the traveling that matters, not the getting there. In this regard, the more unfamiliar the route, the better the trip is bound to be. Successful travel on these soft-surfaced roads requires of driver and passenger only a little native curiosity and a willingness to muddle around in unknown territory.

My own muddling has led me to places in the barrens that still retain its original open aspect—the feeling of spaciousness, of the world having been unroofed. Covering expanses of treeless ground between copses of pine and oak are verdant, shrubby meadows of sweet fern, bracken, danthonia grass, barrens straw-berry, wild strawberry, little bluestem, redroot, and many asters, flea-banes, goldenrods—the list is long. One of my favorites among these is the most widely distributed and certainly best known shrub of the barrens, the wild blueberry.

The barrens of northwestern Wisconsin were known at the turn of the century as the "blueberry basket of the Upper Midwest." Each year field workers made commercial harvests for markets in Milwaukee, Minneapolis, Chicago, and all points in between. These harvests ended with the domestication of blueberries and the sup-pression of wildfire which allowed trees to spread and overgrow most of the meadows.

Despite this loss, and despite the heavy-handed industrial forestry that is practiced there today, many smaller natural open-ings can still be found throughout the barrens which provide an abundance of blueberries. This is good news for sand road travelers and blueberry aficionados alike.

If travel on country roads is slow and deliberate, time stands still while picking blueberries. But I have found this dimension of timelessness to be one of the great benefits of berry picking, particularly for those who, fresh off sun-softened highways, are most in need of slowing down.

It is true that the uninitiated will unavoidably make mistakes, and time spent plucking blueberries could turn into a heinous penance for their sins. Experience is sometimes a cruel teacher.

The worst of these sins, in my experience, is picking on hot, sunny, windless afternoons. This sin is often compounded by an equally egregious error: coming attired in a T-shirt and shorts. Not only will the heat prove wearisome and exposed skin sear salmon pink, but all that succulent flesh will make an enticing meal for clouds of man-eating blackflies—as the harvester becomes the harvested. Under such conditions painful welts will be the only harvest.

Usually it's best to arrive early in the day. Cool, breezy mornings, which help suppress blackflies, provide the optimum conditions for berry picking. So does a little insect repellent applied in the right places, if conditions aren't otherwise favorable. Long pants and a long-sleeved shirt are highly recommended.

Beginners also seem to be rather indiscriminate about where they pick. Upon the first sign of roadside berries the overwhelming urge is to lock up the brakes and begin picking in earnest. This temptation should be resisted unless one wants only a snack.

Look around and find a better place, where the berries are truly plump and abundant. I often find such places away from roads in the partial shade of pines or juneberries, or on north-facing slopes. The effort given to finding these glory patches will be rewarded. Picking will be much easier and sufficient progress will be made to encourage all but the twitchiest individuals to continue. Besides, searching for your own patch has to be one of the best things about blueberry picking—who knows what else might be found along the way?

One characteristic of blueberries might befuddle pickers and even lead them astray. The first time I ever picked wild blueberries I found that some plants held the classic sky blue berries while other plants had darker and duller-looking fruit. Was something wrong with these darker berries? Were they an altogether different type of berry, maybe even poisonous? They tasted like the familiar bright blue, although they were not quite as sweet and seemed to ripen a bit later.

I found the answer in Norman C. Fassett's *Spring Flora of Wisconsin*. It turns out that two distinct species of blueberries grow in our state: the well-known *Vaccinium angustifolium*, or early blueberry, and what I called the mystery berry, *Vaccinium myrtilloides*.

The early blueberry more often grows in the kind of dry, open pine forests that are typical of barrens country. My mystery berry, better known as the velvet-leaved blueberry, is typical of wetter areas, often growing in the company of tamarack and cedar. But it also manages to grow at the extremes of soil moisture, in dry soils and bogs alike. The two kinds of blueberry seem to coexist well in the barrens and appear to grow best in the company of sweet fern, which requires a richer and moister soil.

It seems likely that Native Americans and their ancient forebearers knew all about blueberries and came to the barrens for them. The Ojibway, inhabitants of this area for many centuries, have always had a strong preference for blueberries. In the early 1900s, the renowned ethnographer Frances Densmore recorded details of how the Ojibway harvested blueberries during their annual cycle of harvests.

For untold generations the women and children walked to the barrens country to set up berry camps and spend many a midsummer morning bent low gathering blueberries. Working together in parties, they dropped the precious fruit into small birch-bark baskets, called makuks, which were tied to their waist belts. These were emptied into larger makuks which were carried back to camp. The blueberries were then dried on frames made of slender reeds, or mashed with bear fat and meat to make a kind of pemmican that was stored for use in winter.

Berry harvesting on the barrens has changed greatly since those distant days. I sometimes envy those Ojibway people of old who never heard the rude sound of chain saws somewhere miles off, or whining dirt bikes, or roaring rumbling logging trucks. On the other hand, my ambling twenty-five-mile drive up from Chequamegon Bay and down soft roads to spend a few hours picking just for the sheer enjoyment of it would have been impossible.

For Ojibway women and children a trip to the barrens was not leisure time activity. It was their way to live.

Harvesting wild blueberries is no longer essential to our survival. Yet in the act itself there remains something vital to the human spirit—call it a way of staying connected to our origins in things green and wild. Berry picking seems to be one of the those things our bodies were designed to do well. After all, our opposable thumb and forefinger didn't develop just to flick coins into vending machines. We were berry pickers before we were tool users, and we are still berry pickers today.

In this regard, to think of berry picking as merely an antidote for the pavement mindset is to settle for something less than a full cure. It is not just another of our modern contrivances for "coping" with stress. The necessity of harvesting the wild is more fundamental than that. It emanates from somewhere deep within our being and is pretty much beyond our control—like a genetic flight recorder replaying a pattern of behavior that has been ingrained in our genes since our ancestors stopped sleeping in trees a million years ago.

Whales provide a good, if distant, analogy. Though they live in oceans, whales are air breathers that long ago evolved from a land-dwelling animal. Yet their connection with the windy world above the ocean remains: whales must surface to breathe and survive. Though most of us now live in cities or towns, our home for uncountable ages was a far wilder place. "Wild" is where we came into being and where only relatively recently we have come from. Actively engaging ourselves in wild places is our way of surfacing for air. When we get outdoors and involved in wildness we breathe easier and feel renewed because we have come back to ourselves again in our original home. When we are afraid to get out of our cars, well, maybe that's where the trouble with pavement mentality begins.

Of course there will always be those unbelievers whose misfortune it is to find country roads forbidding and picking blueberries the ultimate in drudgery. That's all right; they can wait where the asphalt ends. Leave the bushes to those who enjoy hunkering low at the end of a sand lane while, berry by berry, the quiet morning hours dwindle away. As nimble fingers become cobalt-stained, asphalt-clad thoughts of elsewhere soon turn dusty, turn to just the task at hand. Shifting their feet a little, the harvesters lift their heads and notice everything. The whispering of a fritillary butterfly's wingbeats. The spicy-sweet fragrance of sweet fern growing stronger as the air warms. Grasshoppers bounding the berry pail. Bluebirds singing their mellow blue notes against an azure sky. The rough, reassuring feel of the blueberry bushes.

There is meaning to be found in picking wild blueberries in the barrens, far from anyone or anywhere. It has much to do with the wonder of the place and with the necessity of the act. And it can be experienced only by those who would travel blueberry roads.

EPHEMERAL, LIKE CLOUDS

I t was early evening, the sizzling end of a muggy dog day in late July. Seeking relief from the oppressive heat, hundreds of people had gone to the beaches on Chequamegon Bay to soak in the ever cool-cold waters of Lake Superior. It had been an unusually hot summer, enough so that some locals had begun talking with expectation in their voices of the coming autumn and the following five frigid months of long johns and Sorel boots.

Like many, I headed down to Bayview Beach for relief from the heat. There doddering along like a sanderling, I wandered mindlessly back and forth from water to beach and back to water again. The heat of the day quickly drained from my legs into the largest inland heat sink in the world and I began spending more time on the beach. After a while I came across spotted sandpiper tracks and small piles of flotsam washed ashore by the last storm, which I idly doted over for a considerable length of time.

At some point—it's a reflex for inhabitants of biting-insect country—I nonchalantly swatted a bug away from my head. But the bug clung to my hand and right away I saw it was a mayfly.

At first this delicate, lacy-winged creature presented a puzzle. I had often encountered mayflies while trout fishing on local rivers. But what were they doing here on the lake? When I looked up and saw that they were everywhere in the air over the water, I realized what was happening: the mayflies were emerging from the lake. That is, they were changing from gilled aquatic nymphs, or sub-adults, into winged, airborne adults. In trout fishing lingo, this was a hatch.

Sitting down in the sand I mentally cast off my own habitual skin of inattentiveness and preoccupation; I wanted to witness this ephemeral event, to see what happens when mayflies hatch from Lake Superior.

Over the water in every direction, mayflies flitted like wet December snow. They didn't spread themselves evenly like some insectile fog, but instead clustered in discrete, cloud-like swarms resembling miniature thunderstorms. Within each swarm there was a continuous circulation of mayflies rising and falling as if flying in updrafts and downdrafts. The scene before me was stupendous— stupendously hard to grasp: millions of adult mayflies were performing their ritual mating flights from one to perhaps a dozen or more feet above the calm surface.

For more than an hour I sat mesmerized. No overt miracles happened; the mayflies didn't appear to increase or diminish in number; they just do-si-doed while this side of the world turned away from the sun. Eventually the sky darkened and people began making their way to their cars. None of them seemed especially aware of this biotic *aurora ephemeralis*, this teeming ritual of raw, fecund life taking place only yards away.

When I left it was almost dark. The swarms had become more condensed and distinct in form, and seemed to be moving inland. When I reached my car they were already above the sand bog that runs parallel behind the beach. In Washburn, four miles south, I found clouds of mayflies haloing street lamps and store lights. At home a few dozen were clinging to the garage door and the back door screen. I carefully gathered a couple of them to bring inside so I could get a closer look and to show Julie and the kids.

At arm's length there isn't much to a mayfly: a tiny head, a thorax with two pairs of frail, wispy wings, and a long segmented abdomen with two or three whippy filaments protruding from the end. But like a fine old watch, only more so, closer examination reveals exquisite beauty and ingenious design. Three pairs of legs are attached at the thorax; the front pair are held almost upright, as if in prayer. The abdomen is long and coarsely segmented, strong yet flexible. Mayfly wings are minutely veined and almost transparent. At rest they are held together perpendicular over the thorax. Their tail filaments are so finely segmented that they quiver in almost undetectable breeze. The color of their exoskeleton usually ranges from pale to dark green.

Scientific nomenclature often reveals one or two key traits of particular plants or animals. *Ephemeroptera* is the name for the order of that group of aquatic insects we call mayflies. The name implies that they are short-lived creatures, but it is really their final adult stage that is truly ephemeral.

Depending upon the species, mayflies may spend one or two years as immature larvae, also called nymphs or naiads, developing slowly and occupying their particular niche on the bottom of a lake or stream. When the nymph is ready to emerge, it swims near the surface as its old skin, or exoskeleton, splits open and the winged adult takes flight. This is the subimago, and it must undergo a final molt of the cuticle covering its exoskeleton (but not its wings) before it becomes a complete adult or imago; this molt happens almost immediately.

Imagoes don't eat; functioning mouth parts were not part of their evolutionary scheme. They carry limited reserves of energy stored as fat and when that's gone, so are they. Adult mayflies have but one purpose in being: to successfully mate and lay eggs. Realizing the utter brevity of their remaining life, usually no more than twenty-four to forty-eight hours, it's no wonder they waste no time in mating. It is an evolutionary fitness test with only two grades: pass or fail.

When the weather and the lake are relatively calm, with mind-boggling synchronicity vast multitudes of mayflies take to the air; how this happens has yet to be discovered. Once airborne, males group together in swarms, flapping their wings to gain altitude, then setting them flat and gliding to the bottom of the swarm. The impression a swarm makes at a short distance is both fluid and chaotic, generative and all consuming. Females hover outside the swarms, then fly into these frenzied bachelor parties and almost immediately depart with a male in tow. After mating, the female flies off to oviposit her fertilized eggs, usually in water or, depending on the species, on submerged vegetation.

The mayflies' fat reserves begin to dwindle and soon they won't be able to fly. If they're not out over water, spent mayflies will cling to whatever surface is available, then slowly fizzle and die. Some species last a few hours longer, others may live a week or more if the weather is cool and cloudy. Hatches can be large or small; many species have several hatches over a period of months, while others hatch just once a year.

If it weren't for lights, probably most people would not take notice of mayflies at all. Light is a powerful attraction for many kinds of mayflies which fly to street lamps on bridges, on docks, and in towns. Come morning, scattered or piled beneath the lights are the bodies of those same mayflies, most already dead. On certain bridges across the Mississippi, mayflies have been known to accumulate in numbers so great that plows were needed to clear them away so cars could get enough traction to move.

About 150 species of mayfly are found here in Wisconsin. Their abundance in streams and lakes is considered an indicator of good to high water quality because they need moderate to high oxygen levels. Taken as a group they are ecologically diverse and fill a variety of niches. For instance, some species are climbers, others bottom sprawlers or grazers or burrowers. The mayflies I brought in the house were burrowers, *Hexagenia limbata*. They thrive in soft mucky bottoms such as are found in many places along the Mississippi and Wisconsin Rivers, and around the Great Lakes, including here in Chequamegon Bay.

Dawn light is always early in midsummer. The air was still, and hazy with humidity. One look at the garage door told me that last night's mayfly hatch was indeed a big one. More than a hundred mayflies held fast to the door, all aligned heads up tails down. They didn't move as I swung the garage door open. The sides of the garage didn't hold a single imago; why they chose the door was a mystery. Better footing, perhaps, or an almost imperceptible night breeze that drove them to seek protection, and the garage door happened to be on the lee side. It seemed worth a small trip around Chequamegon Bay to find out what had become of last night's mayflies.

At the first intersection in town that I met there was a big, old sodium vapor street lamp. No mayflies were in the air, but below the lamp, as I had expected, were many thousands of mayflies, some already flattened by passing cars, the tire tracks easy to trace as footprints in first snow.

Down the street the scene was about the same beneath most of the lamps. The insect layer was thin, a single layer, certainly not a blanket. I began to wonder just how many mayflies had hatched from the bay, no doubt more than I could hope to guess, some unimaginably large number. When I looked elsewhere I found more imagoes that had escaped my attention, littering the sidewalks and parking lots, clinging tenaciously to walls and storefront windows. The shiny pink tiles on Patsy's Bar were glazed with thousands of mayflies. There was no way to even begin to guess how many insects clung to rooftops or hung on to the leaves of trees and plants.

Awestruck, I drove around town, stopping here and there to inspect the carnage, a mass exodus of life energy that quickly waned away before my eyes. I wondered if the big hatch had happened elsewhere around the bay. I turned the car south and drove to Ashland.

Along the way I found only a few mayflies on the road and wondered if the hatch had happened only in the waters near Washburn. But once in Ashland it was obvious that just as many mayflies had been attracted to the lights of town here. Dying imagoes were strewn beneath every street lamp. They clung to storefronts and buildings, just as they did in Washburn. The Dairy Queen was awash with them, and the manager would soon be putting employees to work brushing the insects off windows, walls, and walks. It was difficult to walk without crushing mayflies beneath my shoes. That they would die soon, that many of them were already dead or near dead, didn't ease the feeling I had that I was snuffing out dozens of lives every time I moved a foot. I got back in the car and headed west.

While stopped briefly to gas up at Don's Bait and Gas, I noticed a robin moving between the pumps, collecting mayflies with its bill. Hatches like this must be a real feast for birds, and I began to pay attention to what they were doing. If I had looked sooner, I would have noticed all along that birds were exceptionally active, flitting about energetically. Some herring gulls were even flying erratically, apparently attempting to be flycatchers. In the parking lot of a nearby store several ring-billed gulls were scooping up mayflies. Robins and swallows, which often produce two broods of young, seemed especially busy. But then they are also among the most common nesting birds around the bay. I began to wonder about the mayflies that never made it to land, and of the trout and other fish that must now be rising to take advantage of all the nourishment raining from above. What a feast it must have been.

I might have continued on to Odanah, or perhaps driven north to Bayfield, to see if mayflies had been attracted to the lights there. But I had seen enough of this display of Chequamegon Bay's fecundity. Instead I drove in the direction of home, making my customary stop at Long Bridge, which spans the west mouth of Fish Creek Slough.

I parked my car on the shoulder of the road and walked over to the bridge. Long Bridge doesn't have street lights, but a few mayflies still were hanging on as tenaciously to the old steel girders as they did to life itself. I wondered what impulses might just now be coursing the miniature circuitry of their minds, if they yet remember what it was like to move over the lake bottom, or if they knew how incredibly little time they had yet to live. The prayerful way they faced upward, calmly holding their forelegs as one might fold hands in prayer, seemed to suggest they knew. I picked one up, gently grasping its fine wings, to look closer. The forelegs remained together as if they were glued, throwing doubt on my shaky theory.

Swallows were zooming around the bridge, no doubt filling their crops with imagoes. A soft breeze was in the air, and I took the mayfly I held, lifted it high and let it go. I was surprised, for it flew in the direction of the open bay a short distance before I lost sight of it. No doubt it spent its last moments alive in the waters that gave it life to begin with.

WHERE A HERMIT
THRUSH SINGS

*Morning is when I awaken
and in me there is dawn . . .*

HENRY DAVID THOREAU,
Walden

Too long ago to remember just when, as a young boy I discovered an all but forgotten reach of riverbank woods along the Fox River, near our town in east-central Wisconsin. Not that I was looking for such a place, but the open mind of a child recognized it at once as someplace special.

Countless visits followed that auspicious day. Yet each time I came, I felt as if I were crossing some unseen threshold, as if stepping into another world. Here I was free to play and imagine, to feel the sweep of days and seasons. It was a place for wondering about the lives of white oaks and May apples, toads and chipmunks, clouds and snowflakes—a place of wet feet and bruised shins, of shinnying up shagbark hickories and savoring sweet blackberries. Every living thing in those woods mattered a great deal to me. It wasn't until I left home for good that I realized how, like the flowers and trees, I had rooted and grown in that place.

Over the years I've lived in various regions of the country and found other wondrous parcels of wildness hidden in the folds and recesses of the landscape. But as special as these places were, it seemed I would never find another place that I could know or love so well as my riverbank woods.

Blind luck and a guiding bird changed my mind on this matter. It happened on a soggy morning in late April when I was new to Wisconsin's Lake Superior country. Cold rains had fallen throughout the night. The bedroom window had been left ajar and a rising tide of bird songs awakened me well before 4 A.M.

Out the back door, the weather was a mizzle and the air pungent with rotting leaves and the sweetness of new green growth. It was a morning that seemed well suited for listening and looking for the emerging sounds and sights of spring. With no particular destination in mind, I got in our Honda wagon and headed south out of Washburn.

Driving along Chequamegon Bay, I could already see a faint salmon hue painted on the horizon that signaled dawn's early arrival; the rising sun would shine briefly before being obscured by heavy, gray nimbus clouds. Twenty-five miles later, beyond lowland dairy farms and hay meadows, past sleeping hamlets and woodlots, the road began climbing into the forested Penokee Range.

It was not long after that I began to stop every half mile or so to sit quietly in the car, listening. From a distance came frenzied chirping of chorus frogs, secure in their rain-fed pond. At the next stop, now barely light enough to see, a tail-bobbing palm warbler two-stepped through a patch of alders. Farther down the road, the high, lisping voices of kinglets, pine siskins, and early-arriving warblers filtered down from leafless treetops.

From the car, the warblers, and even the nearest roadside trilliums, were too far beyond reach. It seemed the Honda had taken me as far as it could. Now it was time to disembark into the world, so I set the parking brake and got out.

For the first few minutes, I stood mouse-still, listening to the clear waking sounds of spring woods. Then, with field glasses in hand, I walked up a puddle-ridden logging lane. But I had not gone far before a very different birdsong came looping out of the deep woods. This voice was sweet and melodious, lyrical as a distant tin whistle, yet with jazz-like syncopations and refrains as mystical as an Indian flute. It came as familiar, the voice of an old friend I could not quite place.

Eventually, its lingering refrains and the way its breathy spiraling phrases rose and fell gave it away. It was a hermit thrush, the retiring, clarion-voiced muse of deep and lonely woods.

The thrush's song I found alluring as the mythical pipes of Pan. Why not see where it lives, I thought? So I waded through the red osier lining the ditch and stepped into the woods. As forests go this one was not terribly old, which is to say it had been logged-off sometime earlier this century. I zigzagged my way around sugar maples, basswood, birches, and several large big-tooth aspen that were dying. Within minutes of starting, my pant legs were soaked from thrashing through wet, tangled branches of beaked hazel, red elder, and fly honeysuckle. In scattered openings grew clumps of the earliest spring wildflowers: bluish tufts of blunt-lobed hepatica, twinkling spring beauties, the nodding heads and speckled leaves of trout lilies.

Following ever deeper into the woods, I began having trouble telling where the thrush's voice was coming from. This is a tantalizing, if sometimes frustrating, kind of ventriloquism that is common to many woodland birds. The only certainty is that when their song is loud, the guileful songster is somewhere close at hand.

With only a vague sense of where to go I moved on, trusting the bird would reveal itself. Only a dozen steps more and the forest floor abruptly dropped into a ravine. I started down, but stopped when I noticed something unusual not far ahead. Through leafless maples and birches I saw what appeared to be a tall, dark wall or cliff. After a few more steps I saw that this apparition was actually a grove of exceptionally large conifers holding their ground in the ravine, here in the midst of this logged-over hardwood forest.

The hermit thrush continued its flutey improvisations while I worked my way down to the conifers and then it fell silent. The grove turned out to be a rare remnant of the original Great Lakes forests—a virgin stand of ancient, shaggy-looking hemlocks, with a few giant white pines and stout yellow birches growing among them.

Peering down into the stand I couldn't see very much; beneath the drooping limbs perpetual twilight prevailed. Then out of the corner of my eye I caught a glimpse of motion and, turning my head, I saw what it was: a small, drab-brown bird with prominent black eyes and soft, dark speckles on its cream-colored throat and breast.

It was the hermit thrush. But ours was the briefest of introductions, for it immediately flitted away back into the depths of the stand. Then it began to sing, this time loud enough to startle me as if I had been dozing on my feet. Every subtle inflection in its song was bright as the ringing of small hand bells. I took this as a personal invitation to follow.

Stepping into the dark-shadowed hemlocks was like stepping back in time an hour to early dawn, or many centuries to another age. The ground here was hummocky and almost empty of other plants. Sparse patches of moss and sedge grew on the hummocks and along with them tufts of golden thread, a tiny herb named for the color of its fine roots. A thick, almost spongy layer of needle duff covered the ground. Brittle twigs and small branches lay scattered about.

Near the place where I stood, a wind-thrown hemlock had fallen recently, its trunk and limbs shattered, the sprawling upturned roots still clenching clots of rocky, gray forest soil. Nearby lay several older trunks now decomposing. Elongated mounds of dirt marked where their upturned roots had once been. Young hemlocks, skinny as broom handles and six or eight feet tall, had sprouted atop many of these logs. Rounded, lichen-covered boulders were strewn here and there. I scraped a bit of moss off one and found it was a red volcanic rock, maybe a billion-year-old rhyolite.

Moving deeper into the stand, I found the lowest hemlock limbs were now much higher, fifteen feet or more above the ground. The bare trunks gave the impression of stout pillars supporting the high roof of a dark medieval cathedral. It was quiet as a deep cave in there. Sitting against a hemlock bole, I listened; there were no sounds but my own breathing and heart beating. When I softly cleared my throat, it seemed a rude, almost irreverent intrusion.

Time slipped away in the shadows of that hemlock cathedral. The hours I experienced there seemed to mesh perfectly with the ages. The permanence of the stand and my own sense of impermanence became tangible. Hemlock stands are self-perpetuating, extremely long-lived entities. They may even outlive entire civilizations.

Closing my eyes, I daydreamed back in time, wondering about the birth and life of this stand, and about the early Native Americans who must have strayed through it. I sat stone still there in the company of Longfellow's "Druids of Eld," overwhelmed with a sense of timelessness.

Then suddenly my trance was broken by the song of the hermit thrush. This time I didn't startle, which was fortunate because not twelve feet away, on the same log that I leaned against, alighted the thrush. It seemed to pay no attention to me. Darting to a nearer limb it sang again, unfurling the banner of its voice in long ribbons of liquid sound, setting its timeless phrases free to drift and tangle around the roots and boles of the brooding trees, to curl and fall like threads of quicksilver that dazzle briefly before fading into the needled pools of the ancient forest. Then it spirited away. Minutes later I heard it sing again from somewhere far up the ravine. Then the stand was silent.

Something in that silence told me it was time to leave, that nothing finer could possibly happen this day. Standing and stretching, I looked around one last time. It wasn't a final look, such as is given a place that may never be returned to. It was more a casual "until next time" taking stock of things, the kind of look one might make before leaving a cabin in the woods. For here I had finally rediscovered the legendary threshold of my boyhood riverbank woods, had stepped across and regained a sanctuary out of time where the boundaries of self and place are tightly interwoven. Without a doubt, I knew that I would return here often.

As I backtracked through the woods, it struck me as amazing that despite a century of intensive logging in the Penokees, this hemlock grove had somehow escaped cutting. It showed no stumps, no fire scars, no deer damage to tender seedlings. It had to be virgin timber, yet it was befuddling to try to understand why it was still here. Bad winter weather, a fortuitous mistake by a surveyor, or a never-settled dispute over ownership: any of these might explain the grove's survival.

By the time I reached the road I had already given up on the mystery of the hemlock stand's existence. I was just happy for the serendipity that led me to follow an errant thrush into the woods. Looking back, I half-hoped to catch sight of the drooping tip of a tall hemlock somewhere in the distance. The stand was probably too distant to see, but I looked for a minute anyhow.

Then, just as I was getting into the car, my ears pricked and strained at a final distant sound. It came again faintly as from some far-off daydream, but this time I knew for sure. It was the song of a hermit thrush, singing in a hemlock stand.

THE BIG WALK

The Northwoods holds on to summer for as long as it can. In mid-September, goldenrods in profusion still spread a late summer perfume over frost-licked meadows and roadside ditches. Maples are reluctant to surrender their green and do so grudgingly, just a few leaves turning orange at a time weeks before the inevitable cascade. Chipmunks nap on sunny rocks, then scurry to gather cones for their middens. Sunlight slants lower and more golden as the hours of dark and light briefly run equal. Anxious killdeer begin migrating south in pursuit of receding August weather.

People hold on too, realizing they haven't yet done half of all they had planned to do back in April. New roofs are nailed to old houses in September. Wooden storm windows are finally reglazed, repainted, and rehung. Insulation is added to attics like instant layers of winter fat before the furnace sings of winter again. Gardeners tend their gardens as if it were July, while fretting about the killing frost that will appear any night soon. Evenings see walkers and bicyclists gathering memories that will have to last the winter: the fragrances of mown hay meadows, sounds of wind washing through living leaves, final nighthawk flights.

Like my neighbors I hold on to summer too. For I have warm weather duties yet to perform and unfulfilled dreams and unrequited summer loves to pursue. The duties never go away, no matter the season or how hard one works. If I half-kill myself trying to get ahead, projects and repairs arise spontaneously to fill the void, taking a new and firmer grip on my time. Yet, strangely enough, if I take my sweet time and do only those things that truly need to be done, further obligations are slower to accrue. Time somehow becomes available to pursue those summer dreams.

This year I had dreamed most of taking long hikes in the woods, and in the quiet moments before sleep had often laid plans for cross-country adventure. But as summer progressed these travel plans became merely condensed revisions, a few early morning walks in nearby woods. The first opportunity to hike any significant distance came on Oak Island in August. On an overnight stay there my pent-up desire to "make tracks" resulted in a blitzkrieg of footfalls as I began orbiting the island after my early evening arrival, covering twenty miles of ground before a noon departure the next day. My legs ached and my feet were blistered, but it was a blissful and well-traveled kind of pain. In a few days I was ready to trek again, eager to make scarce in town and spread thin across the country.

A month passed. On a Saturday evening in mid-September, acutely aware of how the final days of summer were sweeping by, I shucked responsibility in favor of unrequited love. Sunday would be the day for a long awaited big walk. And it would happen in a kind of Midwestern hikers' heaven—the Porcupine Mountains Wilderness Park, a few hours' drive east along the south shore of Lake Superior, in Michigan.

Fog nearly fouled my plans. At 4 A.M. it was pea soup outside the bedroom window. The forecast was for humid conditions with a chance of rain and thunderstorms throughout the day. To walk or not to walk, this was a tough question to answer so early in the morning. Years ago, living in the Pacific Northwest, I learned that hiking in the rain can be agreeable, provided one is prepared for the experience. I wanted to hike far in the worst way and feared that another chance to do so might not come again soon. So, I packed a raincoat along with my lunch, water, and notebook. With a hefty mug of coffee and a sweater to fend off fog-shivers I got in the car and drove eighty-five miles through the fog-shrouded Lake Superior lowlands to the Porkies.

By the time I arrived at the Mirror Lake Trail parking lot a breeze had begun breaking up the fog. Rays of warm sunshine came pouring through. A welcoming committee of bright blue asters had taken up residence in the disturbed soil at the trailhead. Shouldering my pack, and without looking back, I strode off through the asters and away down the trail, on my way to a day of constant motion.

At the outset the Mirror Lake Trail is wide and muddy, an old logging road that is used by park maintenance people in their trucks to resupply back-country cabins with firewood. It was dim beneath the forest canopy, like setting the clock back an hour to just before sunrise. As my eyes adjusted I noticed the trees in the forest were mostly yellow birches. This part of the park was logged not long ago—perhaps thirty years—but the regrowth of yellow birch was a hopeful sign, especially because it is so scarce elsewhere in the north country.

The fruits of red baneberry (small white beads at the end of thin red stalks) and false Solomon's seal stared at me like hidden eyes along the trail. One- and two-leaved sugar maple seedlings that had sprouted this summer filled every bare spot between the flowers and shrubs.

From high overhead came the finchy-sounding crescendo, *zeee zeee zeee zeeeee!*, of pine siskins. Crossing a boardwalk over a spring-fed fen the air became sweet with the fragrance of spotted touch-me-nots. Bees were busy, hustling from flower to flower, drunk on nectar and heavy with pollen. Purple finches flitted and called alertly, *pip pip*, their wings sputtering in bursts as if powered by tiny rubber bands. Somewhere in the undergrowth nearby a ruffed grouse warily *chucked*, and retiring song sparrows whispered their thin *seets*.

The rutted road rolled gently with the land the entire two and a half miles to Mirror Lake. It was easy walking in this youthful forest. My legs had found a rhythm and began to loosen up. It was a steady "walk-far-today" pace that matched the dip and rise of the terrain, yet I felt free to stop at any point and listen or inspect whatever caught my attention. It wasn't the usual snail's pace of a naturalist, but the distance I planned to walk today—eighteen miles —was not so far that I had to march with determination in order to return to the car by dark. There would be time to look, but not loaf.

A bridge crosses the Little Carp River near the outlet of Mirror Lake, and this is where the old logging road and younger forests are left behind. This is where wilderness begins. The Little Carp is wide and slow here, part marsh and part stream. Its bottom is covered with speckled alder and big clumps of royal fern, with joe-pye weed filling in between. From the bridge I could see white pines on the west bank towering above a forest canopy of large sugar maples, hemlocks, and yellow birch. It was genuine old-growth northern forest, the *real* thing, the largest and finest of its kind in the entire Midwest.

Stepping from the bridge I heard the sounds of warblers' voices, singing and not just calling. There were myrtle and Nashville warblers and another one that I heard earlier, a black-throated green warbler. Many weeks had passed since the end of the breeding season, and I wondered if the fervor of migration and a dark, foggy morning had something to do with the unseasonable singing and the birds' abandonment of their usual cautious behavior.

Moving off into the forest, I was immediately struck by the astonishing difference in character between old-growth and the younger woods I had just passed through east of the Little Carp.

I had crossed a biological threshold and entered the truly big woods, with huge trees that were widely spaced and with little growing in the understory. A few dozen steps further and I realized I had walked into a cathedral of giant hemlocks; it was dim, as if I had walked under a cloud, and little else was growing beneath the trees. The forest floor was covered mostly with tiny hemlock needles and their miniature cones, and with scattered patches of maple seedlings—not a sapling among them. For a considerable distance sight was unimpeded by shrubs or lesser-sized trees.

As I moved through the hemlocks, to the east I caught glimpses of Mirror Lake, or rather bright reflections off its surface of the gray sky above. It was a big lake, a place that begged to be explored. But it would have to wait for another day. Behind me the first hikers I'd seen this day were approaching, and I moved on.

At the junction with Correction Line Trail, I stopped to check the map and make a final decision which direction to go. The cool forest air was saturated with moisture, and my skin was already beginning to feel clammy with perspiration. Correction Line Trail was less often used and seemed to offer more solitude, so I decided to follow it first. It would join with the Escarpment Trail three miles to the west, which I would follow five miles northeast to the Lake of the Clouds overlook. From there I would again get on the Mirror Lake Trail and hike four miles south, completing a big loop to where I now stood. This last section of trail is more heavily used, and I was saving it for last, hoping fewer hikers would be using it in midafternoon.

Starting off on Correction Line Trail I soon climbed out of the Mirror Lake basin, leaving the big hemlock stand behind. The trail narrowed to a wending path that was wet and muddy in places. The forest was ancient, a common mix of uncommonly large sugar maples, paper birch, hemlock, yellow birch, basswood, and white pines. The hardwoods had long, limbless trunks that "crowned" in a craze of branches far above the ground. Few of the big trees stood perfectly erect; most leaned slightly, their trunks subtly arching or twisting. A layer of younger trees filled the understory, along with hazel shrubs and small hornbeam trees. Herbs of the forest floor bordered the trail, which twisted over rock and root, swung through the trees, and detoured around deadfalls.

The trail and I rolled downhill far through the big woods. Along steeper sections I bounded down the slopes, skipping and feeling like an aging child—a joyous motion that required little extra effort. My mind wandered free as I rambled along, dwelling on good things and bad, sorting out anxieties and blessings, and seeing that, at least at this point in life and especially today, good fortune far outweighed trouble. There are few places better to put one's life in perspective than walking alone on a trail somewhere far out in the big world.

Along the way I began to notice more than a few places where big hemlocks had blown down together. These trees were shallowly rooted, their wide-spreading root wads now standing tall. They were also on a west-facing slope, and perhaps less protected from storm winds blowing inland off Lake Superior. Mountain maple and sugar maple saplings were already crowding beneath the canopy openings left by the blowdowns, each competing for the life-giving light. I didn't notice a single aspen seed or sapling growing in these openings, which are usually the first trees to recolonize openings made by logging. In the long run the sugar maples will win here.

The trail crossed a rivulet with spotted touch-me-nots growing along its course and bluebead lily, wood ferns, and partridgeberry on its banks. It was a narrow, spring-fed stream that fell with a hushed gurgle. A close look at its sandy bottom revealed slender, inch-long cylinders of sand collected in pockets out of the main current. These were caddis fly cases, constructed by the aquatic larvae of an insect familiar to all trout fishermen. I examined a few cases and noticed that each was about the same length and diameter, and made of exactly the same size sand grains. The cases appeared empty and there were no clues to where the occupants had gone. Perhaps they had built larger cases. Or maybe these cases had been cast off as the larvae crawled to the water's surface to undergo their final metamorphosis into winged adults.

The sand in that rivulet drew my eye to the variously colored stones, and the stones brought my attention to the assorted textures and compositions of cobbles and boulders. Some of these rocks were deposited long ago as glacial drift, carried here from far north by the continental glaciers that covered this area as recently as ten thousand years ago. The rocks were an assortment of diorite, gabbro, schists, and gneiss. Some of the surface rocks came from local country rock: basalt billions of years old and full of tiny vesicles that once had been gas pockets in lava; conglomerates, a sedimentary mix of volcanic pebbles that had been deposited with sand and buried deep within the earth; and plain brown sandstone. Native copper was also deposited in large and small masses in this area, and has often been found as "float copper" in river- and streambeds. I wondered if ever there were lucky caddis flies that used inlaid grains of native copper in their cases?

I resumed walking, and soon passed through another large blowdown of hemlocks. Something about the forest floor caught my eye, something about the local topography. The stand was on a sloping terrace, but the floor of the forest was hummocky, with short, linear ridges that more or less paralleled the fallen trees, which were about the same shape and size. I dug into one, kicking the soil with my foot, and found that it contained lots of deep, dark soil— rich in organic matter. It occurred to me that what I was looking at, the topography of this forest floor, may have resulted when large trees blew down or otherwise fell to the forest floor over hundreds of years, each rotting in place and incorporated into the forest floor by insects and worms, right where it fell. I was not sure this was the case, but it seemed plausible.

Merrily strolling along, I came to a larger stream, Land-lookers Creek, which flowed in several gravelly channels. I stopped for a minute to watch a hairy woodpecker hammer on a dead tree, and soon found myself the object of scrutiny of a winter wren. The wren bobbed and darted to and from cover on a deadfall that lay across the stream channel in a bed of spotted touch-me-nots. I had not come this close to a winter wren in years, usually only hearing the diminutive songster or catching a glimpse of it in silhouette. The wren was briefly joined by what seemed to be a migrating flock of hard-to-identify fall warblers. The warblers were actively feeding as they made their way through the forest. Then I turned my attention briefly to the stones in the stream, having float copper on my mind. The gravel was beautiful, a mix of colors and textures. I found a weathered quartz crystal and a pool full of water striders that glided away when I approached. There were no caddis fly cases here, but I found mayfly larvae under some of the larger stones. But no float copper. Just lots of pebbles the color of cinnabar. The stream continued to sing its trickling song, and my heart sang with it as I took my leave down the trail.

The junction with the Carp River Trail came unexpectedly soon. I sat on the trunk of a fallen old paper birch, and took five minutes to check the map and eat a snack. A panhandling red squirrel saw a sucker from far off and soon joined me. I shared my bagel and the core of an apple. According to my map, I was not quite a third the way around the big loop, and I was glad there was plenty of hiking left to do. The sun seemed to shine a little now and then, and so far there had been no rain. I would have lunch atop the escarpment at the Lake of the Clouds overlook, about five miles and two hours of easy walking up the trail. This place was so serene, so peaceful I could have lazed around there all day. Instead, I decided to take the place with me, hold it inside for the day, if not forever.

Carp River was only a few hundred yards up the trail. Spanning the river was a narrow log bridge decked with board, no handrails. Little water was flowing under the bridge this late in the season, but exposed bars of cobble-sized rocks showed that during spring runoff the Carp roars. The highland areas of the Carp receive on average two hundred inches of snow each winter, and when it melts in spring most of it flows right under this bridge and on out to Lake Superior, about four miles west of here.

Crawling down the bank I scrabbled across the bar, again thinking about float copper, but not very seriously. A big dragonfly—it looked like a skimmer—came careening by and crashed into the bridge, then flew off to effect repairs elsewhere. The water was cool, not yet cold. Algae coated the rocks, hiding textures and coloring all a military green. Sweet-smelling goldenrod hung from the banks here. The Carp's character here was long pool, little riffle, long pool, little riffle. I clambered up the bank, waded through a patch of blue cohosh bright with fruit, and moved on.

At first the forest beyond the bridge was predominantly sugar maple and basswood, with hemlocks growing in stands down nearer to the river. But then something extraordinary began to happen. The canopy of the forest remained completely dominated by older hardwoods, but growing everywhere in the understory were countless hemlock trees from seedling to tall sapling in size. I had never seen the likes of this in any other forest. The Porkies have a serious problem with deer overbrowsing the lower elevation hemlock stands near the lake, which are much more extensive in size than these stands. Evidently deer don't use this area for yarding in winter, probably because there is too much snowfall. The soil is hummocky here, and many of the hemlocks grow several in a row on what must have been nurse logs. I hiked along, amazed by what I saw.

This unusual arrangement of trees continued a long way along the trail, in some places more prominently than others. A half mile up trail I found what could be the great-great-grandmother of all of the hemlocks in this area, a towering whale of a tree that was still growing vigorously, not showing the least sign of decay or disease. There were only shattered gray stubs of limbs protruding from the trunk for the first forty feet of its height. Like so many of the other trees on this slope, this one's lower section of trunk curved as if sculpted in a gentle sigmoid shape before running true the rest of the way to the top.

I walked up to the big tree and hugged it, feeling its massively furrowed bark against my cheek. I noted the location of my right hand on the trunk. Then I moved my right-hand fingertips to where my left hand was, moved around the tree and hugged it again. Over a foot remained between my outstretched left hand and where my right hand was originally placed when I first hugged the tree. The span of my arms is about six feet, which along with the extra foot would put the circumference near thirteen feet, and the diameter over four feet. I guessed this ancient tree had to be a hundred feet or more tall. Age would be harder to estimate, but it was probably more than two hundred years. Or maybe much older.

There were some giant, shaggy yellow birches and huge sugar maples nearby, each holding their crown of branches far above the earth. I passed a towering basswood with its mossy trunk widely buttressed in a way reminiscent of cypress trees in southern swamps. It was like a fairyland there, with the trees dwarfing everything. I felt minuscule, and not terribly important among these leviathans. If a faerie flew by, or a large ogre stepped from behind a big tree, somehow it wouldn't have seemed all that surprising.

Somewhere far off a pileated woodpecker laughed wildly, then hammered a message, audibly staking out the area of the forest it considers its own. I wondered if it was aware that, in an ecological sense, it also belonged to the trees. Were it not for this ancient forest, and for the insect life these trees harbored, the pileated woodpecker would not be there. And when it dies, the woodpecker's elements and molecules will disperse back into the soil to be gathered again by the mycorrhizal filaments of tree roots, pulled high into growing cambium of some big tree, and made into leaves or laid down in layers of wood fiber. Other insects will infest the tree and other pileated woodpeckers will consume them. So the life of this place travels full circle.

Remembering that I too had a circle to close, I continued my sojourn through the big woods. Walking along, I realized that I had seen very few fallen trees since crossing the Carp River, whereas on the other side there had been many. The soil seemed to be no different than before; it is everywhere thin and rocky. But the topographic map I carried may have explained why few blowdowns occurred here, and perhaps why that great-grandmother hemlock had survived so long. The prevailing storm winds come from the north or northwest. The hemlock stands I walked through had the benefit of a tall escarpment between them and the prevailing storms. However, trees on the other side of the valley receive very little protection.

The trail continued, slowly gaining elevation as it passed through alternating stands of mixed hardwood and conifer forest, and nearly pure stands of hemlock. There were no signs of deer along the way; no hoof prints, no signs of browsing on young hemlocks, no indication that the hemlock trees here were having any difficulty reproducing.

Some of the rocks in the trail were still sweating; like icebergs their substantial buried portions held the coolness of the subsoil. The air was humid and the day had taken on a dream-like quality. I found myself stopping to stand still in the midst of a hemlock stand quiet as a cave. The only sounds I heard seemed to filter down to me—just the wind's mantra chanting through needle and leaf. Again I felt as if I could stay there all day, but I made a little gesture to honor this place, a little bow, and moved on.

Soon I found myself on a slope that was mostly hardwoods, and which seemed noisy with sound. There were ringing nuthatches, chattering red squirrels, chitting chickadees, screaming bluejays, and the first peal of distant thunder. It would rain that day, but I had brought along a Gore-Tex coat. In the midst of an area where the dark understory was overgrown with whippy young ironwood trees, I notice the breeze had become indecisive, frequently changing direction. Though heavy mist obscured a view of the sky, these signs told of an approaching storm. Within minutes the rain began. It fell not in a downpour, but with just enough intensity for me to put my coat on. It was a mizzly rain, and I liked it.

Soon the trail ran along the foot of a steep slope. Above, there were what looked like short, steep ravines or cuts in the slope with tongues of debris fanning out immediately below each cut. They were an enigma because they were merely gouges that discontinued farther up slope; they didn't appear to be formed naturally. They looked like old mining exploration pits, perhaps remnants from the days when men had hoped to find copper here (the copper-rich ores were found north of here in the Copper Range).

I scrambled up one of the tongues, noting the deep, hollow sounds my feet made. Beneath the thin soil there must have been loose talus of some sort. Yet, if manmade, I could not tell how old these workings were. Large trees grew at the margin of the cut, and the soil appeared old and original across the fan of debris. Only the shape gave it away as something done by the hand of man. But whether it was the result of nineteenth-century miners or twentieth-century B.C. Copper Culture Indians, I could not tell. Since both tread this ground and both extracted copper, only at different times, I wondered if knowing who made these pits would really make any difference. There the mystery remained.

The trail dropped a bit, then climbed, turning in a big loop. In an opening in the woods I looked up and saw tall cliffs whose tops almost disappeared in the mist. I looked down and saw a hiker coming along the trail toward me, the first I had seen since Mirror Lake. They were two women, about my age, wearing big smiles and sporting hefty packs. In passing I greeted them and asked how they like the Porkies. With breathy enthusiasm they said, "Oh, we just love it!"

Climbing through a large stand of hemlocks, the trail swung east, then west, and finally east again. At one point I looked northwest and saw the sky through the trees and realized that I must be hiking across a gap in the escarpment. The trail continued to climb, and I began to notice oak leaves on the trail. Within a few dozen steps I was out of the hemlocks and into a woods full of pin and red oaks, hackberry, and the ground covered with large-leaved asters. Through the trees, to the east I could see a distant forested slope—the other side of the Carp River valley. I was near the ridge top.

There was a flicker of lightning and thunder boomed like a cannon nearby. The rain resumed its gentle patter. I was glad for the coolness of the day and these refreshing showers; if the weather had been hot I probably would have been feeling fatigued. As it was, only my legs were a little trail weary from all the miles I had come. After a few more steps I found myself out in the open, atop the escarpment.

To the east there was a tremendous view, filled with moving mist and the mountains of the Porkies. By geographic definition there is a fine line between low mountains and big hills, and the Porkies are at that line. Inhabitants of larger mountains might be tempted to call the Porkies hills. By Midwestern standards they are mountains, and I accept them as such. Certainly if a pristine wild character counts for anything in a definition of what mountains are, the Porkies would have to rate among the most mountainous of mountains in the northeastern United States.

The view and the unique sense of solitude here were worth savoring. I had hiked a long way and decided to rest and look out over some of the forest I had traveled through. The most famous part of the escarpment, the part with the wonderful overlook of Lake of the Clouds, was still a few miles away. But I preferred this place because I knew it would be more peaceful for the few minutes I would remain there. From where I sat I traced the course of the Carp River, following it for miles where it had carved its way down the forested valley, then turned west and ran out to Lake Superior. Beyond the Carp River the forest was unbroken; the only manmade feature I could see in the distance was the giant ski jump which was near the Black River, at least twenty miles away.

A red-tailed hawk drifted by, and I had the rare opportunity to actually look down on a bird of prey in flight. The big hawk flew northeast and reminded me it was time to also move in that direction. For miles the trail swerved along the edge of the escarpment, sometimes in the woods, sometimes in the open. The plants there were entirely different from the forests below. There were lots of shrubs and herbs: soapberry, juneberry, kinnikinnick, wild rose, ninebark, wild oregano, blueberry. There were also many stunted oaks and wind-deformed pines. The escarpment is a vulnerable edge where the elements beat hard, and on which only the hardiest plants will grow. More than any other place in the Midwest, it reminded me in some ways of sub-alpine areas I had seen in the Rocky Mountains.

Stepping lightly along, thoughts came to mind about the people who must have walked these bluffs long before me. Thinking back to the days of the Anishinabe, before the time Europeans arrived, I recalled that their name for this place meant "crouching porcupine." For them, the Porkies must have been a magical place where *manitous,* or spirits, dwelled. I wondered if the Anishinabe ever held ceremonies on these cliffs, if perhaps their secret Midewi-win Society ever met here. Thinking back further, it is certain the Archaic Indians, the ancient ones who mined copper and fashioned it into implements not far from here, must have traveled these bluffs often. As I marveled at the time sweep of this place, a long roll of thunder resonated across the valley as if to affirm my thoughts.

Too soon I found myself carefully stepping up a badly eroded section of trail, where only tree roots were left running over bare rock. And then came sounds of car doors slamming, engines running, people's voices.

Lunchtime came wrapped in the cool breath of clouds. I took refuge from the tourists below the stone-wall overlook, pulling on a sweater to stay warm. For the time at least, the view of Lake of the Clouds was completely obscured by clouds and mist. I listened to tourists on the other side of the wall grumble or joke about the view. A woman about sixty years old teased her portly husband, telling him she was worried that because he was so front-heavy, a gust of wind might topple him over the edge. A pair of flickers flew by as if on a roller coaster. With bursts of wingbeats and white rump patches showing they bounded up and ahead; tucking their wings, missile-like they dove down in great swoops.

The air was chilly and I began to get goose bumps on my bare legs. I finished my meager lunch, two apples and a bagel, and took a few swigs of water. Reclining on my side I consulted the topographic and park maps. Just six and a half miles remained of my big walk, but they would not be entirely easy miles. The trail down from the escarpment is very steep, and just on the other side of Lake of the Clouds is a serious climb up the west side of Government Peak. My legs were beginning to tire, and I knew from past experience this would be the most likely time to slip on exposed roots and twist an ankle or a knee, or not to lift tired feet high enough and sprain a toe by stubbing a rock. The required discipline for the remainder of the hike was to focus on the trail and be extra careful where I stepped.

Distant thunder continued to roll, and more visitors came to stare out into the clouds. After packing quickly I took my leave, bounding northeast down the trail to a low saddle. From there the trail descended at a very severe angle down the escarpment for perhaps two hundred feet. I picked my way down goat-fashion, stepping or jumping down over loose talus and gravel to little stable ledges. At bottom the trail ran level, then dropped a little through mixed forest to the footbridge that spans the Carp River, not far from the outlet of Lake of the Clouds.

The air was still and full of spicy, peppery odors that reminded me so much of a favorite salt marsh far away in Washington State's Puget Sound. I have never been able to figure out what causes this wonderful smell, but I seem to chance upon it wherever there are sedges and wet, decaying vegetation. Shallow areas of the Carp were full of sedges, grasses, rushes, and other plants: big clumps of royal fern, joe-pye weed going to seed, swamp milkweeds with their long thin follicles full of seeds.

The river was wide there, almost too wide, like an arm of the lake. Crossing the bridge, I looked downstream and saw why the water was high. There was the broad top of a beaver dam that had backed up the river. I could not find the beavers' lodge, but I saw a hefty pile of aspen branches in the water that was probably the beavers' winter food supply. On the other side of the river there were red osier dogwood, smartweed, meadowsweet.

Rain began to fall again, this time in earnest. I put on my coat and began walking briskly. This was a popular section of trail, and it was badly rutted and muddy in many places, which I did my best to skirt. Along the trail not far ahead came a family troop, children, moms, dads, grandfathers strung out in four groups of four or five people each. They were muddy, without rain gear, and obviously wet. One of the grandfathers told me they were coming from Mirror Lake, where the seventeen of them spent two nights in an eight-bunk cabin. They all seemed to be in good spirits, though someone from each group I passed asked me how much farther it was to the end of the trail, which I presumed meant Lake of the Clouds.

Not a hundred paces behind the last family group came three fishermen carrying bait buckets, fishing rods, and tackle boxes.

They were about the same age as I, and all sweating profusely under their nylon caps with trucking emblems sewn in front. They obviously had walked a long, long way with armloads of gear. They were also obviously without a map. With a southern drawl one of the men asked me how far it was to the lake. Another recounted that their friend, the one with the sheepish grin, had told them he knew a shortcut through the woods to the lake. Which lake they couldn't say. They also said they had been walking for many hours and that their truck was parked back near Government Peak. This was impossible; the nearest parking place to Government Peak is the Mirror Lake trailhead, five miles back up the trail. Assuming they were looking for Lake of the Clouds, I told them they didn't have far to go. Smiles of gratitude lit their weary faces. One of them said, as they departed, that they would walk the road from the Lake of the Clouds overlook back to their car instead of hiking all the way back through the forest. I did not have the heart to tell them that it would be easier to follow the trail back; by road the distance was more than twenty miles. "Live and learn," is what my Dad always said.

Moving on, the trail entered a stand of hemlocks, and then steepened enough that I began breathing deeply as I tried to keep up a good pace. The trail soon ran close to a spectacular, deep gorge that had cut down into solid rock. It showed up on the topographic map as a severe uphill warp of otherwise serene contour lines. Small trees and shrubs grew out of cracks in the mossy rock walls of the gorge. Ferns, mosses, and liverworts clung to all available surfaces.

There was also a continuous sound of water spraying as the small stream in the gorge fell over ledges and large, broken blocks of wall rock. The declivity was so regular in width and so straight that I half-guessed it represented a weakness in the country rock, a vulnerable line where water found it easier to have its way—most likely a fault.

Near the top of the small mountain the slope relaxed and the forests once again became predominantly hardwood. My legs were sore, but I was relieved that the hardest part of the trail was now behind me. Walking on more or less level ground was also a relief for my sore feet and ankles which had been stubbed and strained too much. I ambled along, careful of where I placed my worn-out feet but otherwise feeling pretty good. In fact, I began to think that I was feeling too good, that I was on some kind of walker's high, the prostaglandin hormones or some other hormones perhaps numbing my body and allowing me to enjoy the final miles of the big walk. Atonement for my sins, in the form of aches and cramps, would surely come that night or the next day. But at the time I found this difficult to worry about. When a person's spirit wants to soar, who in their right mind would try to stop it? An ovenbird began singing and all I could do was smile.

At the high point of this section of the Mirror Lake Trail the forests changed in composition again, this time to very young trees in a matrix of tall shrubs. To me, it looked like the regrowth one sees after a clear-cut, but I knew this could not be the case here. The area had blown down or otherwise burned in a severe fire; I could only guess what happened.

Moving up the trail, the forest again turned old, this time to large basswoods, red maple, black ash, and a few white cedar scattered about. This was a wet assemblage of trees found where the soil is often wet through the growing season. From somewhere in the forest an eastern gray tree frog momentarily *chirped* its mating call out of season, reinforcing the feeling of wetness this place had. Before moving on I looked down and found wild ginger growing profusely. I pulled up a short piece of its running root, cleaned it, and popped it into my mouth. Though I was not fond of ginger, the root tasted like the real thing.

Soon I was moving through lower areas with sloping terraces full of big hemlocks again. After crossing a few small streams I finally came upon Mirror Lake and a large log cabin that was shuttered and locked tight. The air smelled of damp wood smoke, and a fire ring full of ashes was all that remained of that family troop's breakfast campfire. A few steps more and I was once again at the junction with Correction Line Trail, having come around circle.

Standing there a minute I tried to reflect on the day, to pull together some significant reflection on my walk, maybe think of some small ritual I could perform. But I came up empty. All that I had seen and felt would come home with me, there to consider and reconsider, to keep in my heart and mind. At the moment I just felt lucky that this wonderful wilderness remained intact and that

I had two good legs to carry me through it. My feet ached when I stood still, and I was anxious to begin walking the remaining two and a half miles to the car.

Leaving the last of the big hemlock stands behind, I crossed the bridge over the Little Carp River, this time not pausing to savor the view. On the other side, a scurrilous red squirrel scolded me from high in a red oak. From there I rolled along and my mind began drifting away from my surroundings and back to home and family. As I walked the now truck-rutted trail I casually gazed about the forest. Somewhere along the way I found the remains of an orchid I had missed on the way in, a rattlesnake plantain that had gone to seed. Another tree frog called. Tips of buried boulders protruding through the trail were still sweating.

It was one of the last days of summer, and I was on the final stretch of my big walk. It seemed that summer and I were on a parallel course, having come this far together to some conclusive ending. When I reached the car, summer in the Porkies was over for me. The next time I tramped these trails, night frosts had greeted leaf and limb. Leaves had lost their chlorophyll, turning various shades of gold, orange, and yellow as they fell. The flickers were long gone, no flowers bloomed, no tree frogs with their rickety call. The only voices were those of winter birds and wind clattering the bare bones of branches together. It was a new season in the Porcupine Mountains, and yet another time to walk in the wilderness.

A FINE MADNESS

When it gets hard to stop fishing, even on woolly November days when northeasters churn Lake Superior to spindrifting rollers, when your fingers are chilblained and the only way to keep the combers from over-topping your waders is by jumping—when it gets *that* hard to stop, it may be too late for you.

All the more so if you've been flinging spoons into the rollicking surf all morning without once feeling the tug of a brown trout or coho, and *still* you find it hard to take your leave. No doubt the numbness in your legs has worked its way up to your head. Better get ashore while you can, pull off those miserable waders, and find that thermos you'd forgotten about hours ago. It's time to count your marbles again, just in case.

Shorecasting for fall-run coho salmon and brown trout on Lake Superior is as fine and weird a madness as anyone could hope to be possessed of. Few recognize it as such, but it is actually a harmless form of seasonal lunacy. Acute symptoms begin to appear sometime in mid-September.

Stopping by one of the sandy beaches around the Bayfield Peninsula one afternoon you notice how serenely inviting the lake looks. Someone out there in a small aluminum boat is trolling. And

then a large, silvery piscid launches itself skyward at a distance that appears to be just beyond casting range of a person in chest waders standing tiptoe. It was a rather impressive leap to boot.

Moments of simple calculation and rapid fermentation follow. As night falls those fish will move closer to shore, certainly within casting range. There's still time to get your tackle and return. And that's just what you do.

The water is more than a little cold, and right away you regret wearing only jeans under your waders. Sunshine on your shoulders helps a little, but evening is coming fast. It's funny how the world can look so summery with the lake already chilling toward ice. But it's not intolerable, so you begin casting your two-thirds-ounce chartreuse and hot pink and trouty-looking spoons. Spoons like modern art, intended to elicit immediate gut reactions.

You keep zinging the spoons out as far as your eight-foot rod will launch them. Ever so slowly the sky starts fading to that inky blue that says a clear, cold night is coming on. And for the longest while, nothing happens.

But then, almost inevitably, there comes a no-nonsense boil and a fierce tug on the line that clearly means business. Luckily, you remember to set the hook and something powerful makes your rod tip dance a fast cha-cha while the drag sings falsetto. On the first jump you see it, a nice coho fresh in from the expanses of the lake, silver sides still flashing bright, maybe four pounds.

From the start you can tell this salmon has inherited all the essential moves and tricks to shake loose a spoon, first charging then tail dancing and whirling like a dervish. This goes on for maybe a minute before the hook abruptly pops loose, which happens often enough. But that's O.K. because you got most of the fun and would have let it go anyhow. There will be more fish, and later you'll keep one to take home and broil.

And so the fall madness begins. Next morning you're out there just as first light begins dabbing the coal black sky with faint hues of watermelon. Later in the day there will be plenty of boats trolling back and forth out in front, some weaving uncomfortably close because they believe you're onto fish, which may or may not be the case. By comparison, shorecasting hasn't exactly been a burgeoning sport along the south shore of Lake Superior. But most weekdays and even some early mornings on weekends you'll find yourself alone in the shallows.

Like right now. You have the lake and sky to yourself. The brightest stars adorning January skies now twinkle and glimmer through the hazy half-light of September morning. The vast and dark, calm water seems viscous as oil, practically molten. In the blackness you cast and cast again. The water is heavy and you can sense the massiveness of the lake as it moves and presses against your legs and belly. Mergansers come scudding by low and fast, silhouetted against the eastern sky. As the morning aurora brightens, a light-hearted giddiness fills you, an old happiness from tender years. And then, just as you're preparing to make your next cast, thirty-some yards out something big rolls at the surface.

So the season progresses, from green to gold of leaf, to no leaf at all. From days when fish are "in," to others when not a single message comes down the telegraph line. The stuff you wear to stay warm under your waders changes radically. From relatively breezy stuff like thrift shop jeans you progress to every polar item you can beg, steal, or borrow. Hands chafe, fingers harden, skin splits. Literally to save face you stop shaving. By early November, a rather amazing transformation has occurred.

And just in time. For this is when shorecasting reaches its absolute finest. Now the infamous gales of November begin to appear, with billowing zephyrs of wind, rain, sleet, and snow that churn the lake to a wildness that is hard to imagine. But if you're up for it, it's a wildness you can experience.

Get a good rain coat and button it tight from your chin down over your waders. Then, when the big waves are quartering into the beach, edge out into the surf as far as you dare. Start casting, see what happens.

Old-timers say the "best" shorecasting happens when heavy winds are pushing big waves ashore. Some say bait fish are herded into the shallower water; others say that the pounding action of the waves near shore heightens the urge to spawn in salmon and trout. No one knows for sure.

But maybe the old-timers had something else in mind when they said "best." Maybe it has more to do with just standing out there swaying in the surge and pull of Gitche Gumee, to have a rogue roller catch you by surprise as it breaks over your shoulders, to be caught up in the sound and the fury of all that primal wildness, if only for a little while.

It's at about this point that catching fish becomes secondary. Sure, before you're done there's a good chance that something with a spirit to match that of the lake will latch on to the end of your line. But even if you don't catch a fish, make no mistake about it: This *is* fishing. And the only way you can experience such a fine madness is to give it a try.

GRASPING A BIRD LENS

Autumn is a season of loss, a draining away of life from the land that is at once awaited and familiar, yet in some ways darkly saddening. Maples flame like hopeful bonfires, then stand naked and forgotten. Frost sparkles as it grimly reaps meadow and marsh, grasshopper and dragonfly. Cold fogs blanket the year's aging skin, portending colder, whiter sheets that will soon cover the land. Evenings turn dark and quiet by seven, then six. The nighthawks have already gone, and the swifts as well. Daylight slants low, then lower still, bending light into mellower tones hinting of winter's long twilight. The melancholy of autumn is that most of the beautiful days come early and depart all too soon. Then follows the slow withdrawal of life, a gray withering of the once green land that lasts until snows cover all.

When does autumn begin and when does it end? Our dependence on the celestial calendar for an exact date and time obscures the true nature of seasonal change. An exact time when one season surrenders to the next is impossible to put a finger on. This is because such a thing doesn't really exist. We have drawn and quartered our year by equinox and solstice, and in the process limited our understanding of seasonality to mere astronomical definition.

Nature proceeds according to its own rhythms, has many clocks by which all living things ebb and flow in accordance with latitude and the eccentricities of both global and local climate. No one would question the fact that the tilt of the earth and its elliptical orbit around the sun are the reason we have seasons. But the earth's tilt and elliptical orbit are the flywheel and not the precise regulators of seasonal change. The timing of seasonal events is everywhere a secret—the ineffable rhythms and reasons shared by living things. It is the unpredictable interplay of life and land with the vast and world-shaping forces of the oceans and atmosphere.

Instead of cosmic switches tripped at quarterly points in the path of the Earth's orbit—Voila! Another season!—seasonal change proceeds as a cycle, a grand, slow unfolding and meshing of an almost infinite number of smaller events. It is everywhere just one thing after the next. Seasons come by flower blossom and insect buzz, by leaf fall and hibernation, by snowfall and winter kill, by the green of bud and seed germination in warm, musty soil.

The new science of chaos holds that very small changes are important because they can have tremendous influences on much larger events. The fluttering of a butterfly's wings in China could determine the weather next month in Wisconsin, or even the procession of events through an entire season. Holding to the old celestial definitions of seasons is comforting and convenient as a particular way of referencing events in the world. But it is accurate only in a general way. Our sense of seasonality is a manifestation of both our way of seeing the world and our concept of time. Newton's three-hundred-year-old mechanistic way is still our way and Einstein's relativism has yet to take hold. Chaos may take even longer before it becomes a part of our way of seeing the world.

As when we consider the onset of love, precision fails us when we try to say when a season begins, and when it ends. A love or a season: it is a series of unforeseeable and never fully understood events that lead us to a place and a condition. It could be that certain feeling we get in the presence of another that first makes our heart go "ping." It could be everything that brought us and the world to this day, and the sweet scent of crushed tansies where we stand picking apples in early October. This is autumn, we say.

Yet we persist in our old way of seeing seasons as something wholly discrete. In doing so the full measure of a season slips through our fingers. In the way that only lovers can hope to know what love is, perhaps only physicists, shaman, and native peoples are prepared to know the true nature of seasons.

It is interesting that the native Ojibway people have always regarded the year more broadly. Since their early origin they have had names for six approximate seasons, and operated on a lunar calendar. Their intimate association with the landscape and the occurrence of natural events was, and remains, crucial to their way of life and the survival of their culture. The traditional harvest of Manomin—wild rice—has always been an important event that occurs when the season, the weather, and the rice plant itself all conspire to ripen the grain. The time of ripening is an imprecise thing, varying somewhat from year to year and from place to place. But this variation never has mattered very much to the Ojibway. They have always observed the many changing conditions, and when the rice was ready they simply harvested it. The most important thing was that there was rice. And so their sense of seasonal events was woven into the very fabric of who they are as a people. They are careful observers of the world. What has always mattered was not the precise time a thing happened, but simply that it happened. And so they have always paid attention.

Birds are another kind of living proof of the untimely nature of seasons. If bird migration is a sign of spring and autumn, as is commonly held, then least sandpipers appearing on the Long Island beach in mid-July—only days of rapid flight away from their sub-arctic nesting grounds—have to be among the first signs of autumn here in Chequamegon Bay. Yellowlegs and other shorebirds follow in a few days, their appearances further evidence that the autumn migration has begun. If one insists on the traditional notion of what a season is, this makes for an awfully short summer.

The trickle of autumn migration continues to grow until it is a stream, then a river that will all too soon run dry. Indeed, by the time of the celestial autumnal equinox, when the Earth reaches that position in its orbit where the sun appears to move below the celestial equator, many of the nesting songbirds in the bay area have already taken flight for warmer climes. Before the leaves of shrubs and trees even begin to withdraw their sugars and green chlorophyll, leaving the brightly colored pigments behind, birds from boreal Canada are already arriving to take up winter residence here. As the season progresses and the weather becomes more severe, hardy common goldeneye ducks show up in the bay in mid-October and remain until freeze-up; a few are usually seen during the Christmas bird count.

Perhaps it is this ongoing nature of what we call "bird migration" that can help us see seasons as a continuous intermingling of changing events.

The irregular phenology of birds arriving and departing here in the Chequamegon Bay area is another example of the interplay of events and the continuity of seasonal change. Ornithologist Dick Verch, a professor at Northland College in Ashland, has recorded dates of bird arrival and departure for more than a decade around the bay area. His observations show the range of days a particular kind of bird could be expected to arrive or depart. But a precise date or time cannot be placed on a calendar. Every year and every day of every season is different. According to Professor Verch, "most" cliff swallows have departed the bay by mid-August, even though the weather is still warm and insects abundant. Northern orioles are "usually" gone by September 1. The few blackpoll warblers he sees each fall have been almost, but not always, observed within two days of September 20. The last of the wood thrushes, which breed here, will have departed by mid-September.

The last sighting of flocks of migrating bluebirds is usually before September 30. Gray-cheeked thrushes are most often seen passing through during the first week of October. Fox sparrows arrive very near October 10, and remain in the area for about two weeks. The last loon will be seen in the Chequamegon Bay in early November.

As with wild rice and the Ojibway people, the important thing to realize about bird migration is that it is both ongoing and imprecise, and that it takes place in a world that is ceaselessly shifting and changing. But the most important thing about bird migration—and autumn—is that it happens.

So it is that the birds migrate southward from the north country landscape in autumn. They come in great waves and small pulses and on any given day songbird flocks could be flitting through trees, shorebirds dashing along beaches, or a solitary bird garnering a few seeds at the edge of a meadow. In the country around Chequamegon Bay, the chances of seeing any of the birds Professor Verch has listed on a given day are largely determined by the vagaries of the weather, the kind of habitat in which one is bird-watching, and the unpredictable chance that a flock of migrating songbirds happens to be in the vicinity.

There is one place, however, that by its unique location concentrates fall-migrating songbirds in great—at times incredible—numbers. This extraordinary place is a large sandspit located on the south tip of Outer Island which, at eight thousand acres, is the second largest island in the Apostle Islands National Lakeshore.

Outer is important to these migrating songbirds, hawks, and falcons during both spring and fall migrations, though the number of songbirds is much greater in the fall. In the late 1970s, Jim Harris and other biologists observed and recorded the great numbers of birds that used the island as a stopover. But Outer Island is remote and not an easy place to get to, especially in autumn when high winds and squalls make travel to and from the sandspit difficult and often impossible. It is because of this that few people, mainly biologists and some birdwatchers, know about Outer Island and its importance to migratory birds.

About seven years ago the natural resource manager at the National Lakeshore started a program designed to monitor migratory songbirds on Outer Island. The results from the first autumn more than confirmed the earlier studies. Through careful counting it was found that more migrating songbirds concentrate on Outer Island than anywhere in the Upper Midwest. Here hundreds and sometimes thousands of migrating warblers, finches, sparrows, thrushes, bluejays—more than a hundred species of birds—can be seen in migration from late August to early October.

It was the best of luck that I got the chance to go to the Outer Island sandspit one September to help with the migratory bird survey for a few days. At six in the morning I found myself sitting low in the beach grass. From there I would see and count all kinds of songbirds, hawks, and falcons flying both high and low. They would be traveling in small bunches of twos and threes, by dozens in flocks, and at times by the hundreds. That clear morning I did not have to wait long before birds started flying over as they left the island. There were flocks of robins, thrushes, bluejays, sparrows, finches, thrashers, catbirds, flickers and more. As the flow of birds picked up, I counted them by fives and tens and twenties. I was counting fast, calling out numbers and, when I could identify them, the species, to my field assistant who recorded the information in a field notebook. Loud squawks often came from the pines where merlins were chasing down flickers. Sometimes peregrine falcons came racing by after both merlins and flickers, terrorizing birds, then breaking off the chase at the last minute. I watched one peregrine at a great height repeatedly dive or "stoop" like a stunt pilot on flocks of flickers trying to gain altitude as they left the island. The scene was a wild circus the likes of which I had never before seen. By nine o'clock the number of birds leaving the island had dwindled to a trickle. Sitting in the grass, I was almost numb with awe. I had counted thousands of birds and witnessed a tremendous expenditure of life energies as they launched themselves on an odyssey that will take them hundreds and thousands of miles south. Many of the warblers and vireos would travel as far south as the rainforests of Central and South America. I was glad to be there watching them as they departed, but I felt a little sad wondering what might become of them.

It is no real mystery why so many birds pass through the environs of Outer Island. Many kinds of songbirds really don't like to migrate over large bodies of water. Daytime migrants, because they can see where they are traveling, rarely are enticed to cross Lake Superior. But night migrants can, and often do, begin to cross the lake without realizing it. Come dawn, when these night migrants find themselves stranded high over Superior, they instinctively fly in the direction of the nearest landmass they can see. Birds that had headed out over the water only shortly before daylight may actually turn around and fly back to the north shore. For others already far out over the lake, the only option is to continue their flight southward to the nearest landmass along the south shore of the lake.

For many night migrants crossing western Lake Superior, Outer Island—which of all the Apostle Islands reaches farthest out into the lake—is the nearest landmass they can see. By virtue of its location Outer acts like a great convex lens, gathering wayward birds from a wide expanse over the lake and bringing them to a place where they can rest and feed before again dispersing in their southbound migrations. The focal point of this great bird lens is the sandspit.

The Outer Island sandspit is one of those rare places where a hand can be laid on the great pulse of autumn and one can actually feel the season change as it takes flight from the northern landscape. Outer's sandspit is a place where that wild, primal urge to migrate can be experienced. There it is not vicarious, some vaguely held notion ruminated upon from an easy chair. There, and perhaps only there, it is a *felt* thing, like the warmth of an old fire fanned hot in the dark, like a deep longing in the hollow spaces of one's bones. Standing on that sandspit with birds streaming by in farewell flight to the mainland and places far beyond, the overwhelming urge is not to ponder or wonder, not to linger or go home. It is autumn, and in your heart the singular, deeply felt sense is to follow.

OLD MAN RIVER

One morning I awoke before dawn, as I sometimes do, to take advantage of this quiet time to write. For a while I tried to work, but I felt restless and distracted. Finally, I went over to the window to look out at the world. It was early October, cool and windy, with a harvest moon falling through a cloudless sky.

From our second floor window I had a small view of Chequamegon Bay between trees and a few hundred-year-old brick buildings on Bayfield Street. The scene was luminescent with moonshine and dawn light already rimming the eastern horizon. Southeast beyond the wave-swept bay swam the low, sweeping Penokee Range. In the eerie light they appeared as thin wavering brush strokes of milky blue hills, a distant ghost range drifting between penumbral sky and quiescent lowland forests. Atop one distant hill a radio tower beacon winked like a signal fire.

My mind moved to water and the countless rivulets and streams flowing down from the Penokee Mountains to Lake Superior. In the way branches and limbs join in a hardwood tree, these streams come together to form the Potato, Brunsweiler, Marengo, and White Rivers. Once out of the Penokees they flow across lowlands, cutting deeply in soft, iron oxide-laden glacial lakebed clay laid down nine thousand years ago. It is here these rivers, along with the Kakagon, join the "trunk" of the tree, the Bad River, which empties into what many wetland ecologists believe to be the largest freshwater estuary in North America, the Kakagon–Bad River Sloughs Wetlands complex.

A significant part of this watershed is encompassed by the Bad River Indian Reservation, a three-hundred-square-mile block that was reserved for the Bad River band of the Lake Superior Ojibway nation in treaties made in the mid-1800s. This land has never been owned by the United States government, though early on the Ojibway had leased or sold rights to more than forty percent of it to timber interests, and much of this land has already been logged.

Gazing across the bay, I daydreamed awhile about the White River, mused over memories of maps I had seen. Someone once told me the stretch of the White flowing through the reservation is still wild. A friend who had canoed through it said, "Man, it's like being in the middle of no place I'd ever been before." His only proviso was that "two power lines and a gas line cross the river, but otherwise you're out there." There would be no roads, houses, clearcuts, or other artifacts of human habitation or habituation. My friend said it would be rare to see other people out there. He thought the river went too deep into the heart of the place for most people to want to go there without a good reason.

The White River is famous among trout fishermen and whitewater enthusiasts. But this fishy and frolicsome reputation is earned upstream, where it tumbles and swirls over glacial till and bedrock. Through the reservation it maintains its swift current, but there is no whitewater. The river's hydrology changes markedly as it begins to meander in rhythmic undulations, easily cutting away the soft clay bank here, depositing a muddy bar there. Instead of flowing clear it often runs as thick and muddy as the Missouri River. By the old laws of gravity and fluid dynamics the White confines its meandering habit to the floor of a valley that swings in a great arc from east to north en route to its confluence with the Bad River in historic Odanah.

"White" seems a misnomer, at least for this lower portion of the river. The Ojibway must have a more appropriate name for it, but I haven't been able to track it down. My friend calls it Old Man River, which seems fitting enough.

To canoe Old Man River had been one of my ambitions of the past summer. But desires have a way of being supplanted by duties, or at least by other desires. Twice I made plans to go, only to have them thwarted. Now it dawned on me that this day would probably be as good as any to make a trip down the White. Recent heavy rains had ended and clear, windy weather was forecast. That this might be my last opportunity of the year provided the final justification.

It was nearly noon when I slid the canoe I had rented into the water below the Highway 13 bridge that crosses the White River south of Ashland. Already I had misgivings about the so-called solo canoe I had rented. It was flat-bottomed, fourteen feet long, and looked more like a heavy two-person pleasure craft. But I was eager to see the White River country and decided the extra work it would take to maneuver and portage a heavier canoe around and over log jams would be worthwhile.

After putting the canoe in I shoved off into the strong current and felt it suddenly sweep the canoe away. The river was running high and swift from a month of above normal rainfall and recent heavy rains, and it literally sucked my boat downstream. East of the highway a high, arched concrete railroad trestle reminiscent of a Roman aqueduct spanned the river. The bridge had been built long ago and was now abandoned. Blocks of the crumbling arch have broken away and fallen into the river. In times of low water the blocks almost form a weir over which the river pours. But now the river was several feet higher and the canoe easily swept over them and onward through the cavernous arch.

From here the river swings sharply north and drops a few feet where battered wood pylons from an older wooden trestle protrude a few inches above the purling water. I intended to follow the bend close to the inside to avoid some midstream standing waves—signs of boulders lying below. But as I began turning the canoe it responded too slowly. In seconds I was stuck atop a submerged boulder just upstream of the pylons. The unstable canoe immediately canted over, and once water began pouring over the gunwale the boat obliged by tipping even farther. Before it swamped completely I abandoned ship. Holding it by the stern I dragged the canoe onto a shallow midstream gravel bar where I struggled to tip the water from it.

As I stood there soaked to my waist with the river just racing by, my enthusiasm for the trip was suddenly dampened. My clothes, pack, and notebook were soaked. And what I struggled to hold was not a canoe but a rudderless, two-person bathtub with which I hoped to negotiate twenty or more fast, meandering, windy, snag-ridden and logjam-blocked miles of Old Man River.

Why am I doing this? was a natural question, but I couldn't think of an answer.

I had hiked in this area before and knew that beyond the next bend a wooden snowmobile bridge spanned the river. From it there was a trail back up to the highway. It marked the point of no return. From there to Odanah no other bridges crossed the river and no roads skirted near. I stood on that gravel bar awhile trying to recall what problems my friend might have encountered, but none came to mind. I knew that once I was beyond the bridge there was no way I could paddle, push, or pull such a bulky canoe back upstream against the current. I would be committed to the journey.

Prudence had never been one of my stronger virtues. Intrigue won out and I decided to go for it anyhow. I was wet but warm and trusted the judgment of my friend who assured me that beyond the snowmobile bridge there was no fast water to contend with, just logjams to get around. My dunking was an early lesson in caution. I drained my pack and tied it to a thwart, then shoved off with a hoot into the current again. The river cradled the stubby canoe and swept it along like a leaf downstream toward wilder country. A canoe hewn from a log, I imagined, wouldn't handle much better.

Beyond the wooden bridge the river bent sharply south and entered a long tree-lined corridor. The limbs of the taller trees tossed back and forth in long, sweeping arcs by the hard, gusty winds which had begun to blow. Far aloft roaring winds prevailed from the west. But at the bottom of this steeply cut valley wind came swirling every which way, ricocheting off steep hillsides and cut banks, caught and deflected up- or downriver by trees on either side.

Trees in fall colors crowded the clay banks. Tall leaning silver maples with multiple trunks were most common. Most of their leaves were a luminous pale yellow, as if they glowed from within. But for reasons unknown a few of these maples had leaves that were still green and healthy, as if summer was lingering nearby. Silver maples are uncommon this far north and the White River is unique in harboring the northernmost natural population in Wisconsin.

As I was swept along I noticed places where large, dead trees with gracefully arching, broken limbs stood like barkless, petrified giants above the lowland forests. These were the decaying bulwarks of American elms. Once common, they were destroyed by the pervasive Dutch elm disease over the past thirty years. Beneath them were thickets of box elders, their tangled limbs holding but a few unsplendorous yellow-green leaves. In other places black ash, the first hardwoods to drop their leaves in autumn, crowded together nakedly in pure stands.

Where the river ran against banks or hill slopes, dense stands of white cedar threw deep shadows, or stands of white and red pine mingled with sugar maple and paper birch. Most of the ravine crests seemed to be capped by tall pines or big tooth aspen groves, their toothy leaves shining tawny gold.

Slowly the river channel began turning more often, sinuously folding back and forth on itself in widening folds. More than a lesson in river hydraulics, this was an opportunity to feel nature's propensity for repetition and rhythm. Views ahead became progressively shorter. The speed of the current and attention needed to negotiate obstacles and bends allowed only enough time to recognize, but not to memorize, the countless details passing by. There was time to bear witness but not play a significant role in the living and dying and changing of things here. A glacial boulder, one maple leaning farther over the water than the others, pine needles and leaves drifting in the current, a logjam, the noticeable absence of people and their artifacts—these are the things the river allowed my mind to settle on.

Paddling downriver with the sun streaming and wind blowing, maneuvering the canoe constantly, I was lost in the details of the landscape. Somewhere along the way time and distance began to escape me. My only sense was that it was early afternoon. I never wear a watch because I have always broken them. But mainly I don't wear a watch because most of the people I know who do wear one are overly time-conscious. Timeliness is but a kind of consideration, and pondering the future an occasional necessity. But the present moment is where I like to spend most of my time.

Daniel Boone-fashion I could make a fair guess of the time and how far I'd come, if I really wanted to. But my early anxiety was gone. All I knew and cared about was that I was moving down a wild river, somewhere between where I began and where I would end this voyage. That was time enough for me.

Swinging around a hairpin bend, the river suddenly disappeared. In its place was a monstrous snarl of silvery-gray weathered and busted tree trunks and limbs, with a few pieces of tattered brown plastic snagged here and there as a reminder of who lives upstream. The river flowed under the logjam and a portage was unavoidable.

My first inclination was to cross the jam itself. But the floating logs at the upstream edge promptly submerged when I tested my weight on them—not a good idea. Back-paddling, I made my way to the less steep left riverbank where handfuls of sedges greeted me. I scrambled up the bank and into the brush, then slowly dragged the heavy canoe up over the lip of the bank. Fortunately, it was not a long portage around the jam; dragging an eighty-pound plastic bathtub through dense brush was hard work. That no portage trail existed there was evidence of how little use this stretch of the White receives.

Before putting in again I took a short hike. Everywhere ferns and nettles lay dead or dying, victims of recent frosts. Their foliage was mottled yellow, umber, cinnamon, and pale green. The fertile fronds of ostrich fern stood erect above the wreckage of colorful leaves on the ground—pale and bright yellow of silver maples, burnt orange of sugar maple, rust orange and burgundy of red oaks, Chinese red of red maples. A rivulet cut a deep, two-foot-wide notch across the floodplain. The only sound there was the rush of wind shifting through leaves and branches, and the purling of the river flowing under the logjam. So far I had not seen or heard any birds and the woods here seemed empty of animal life. The air was fresh, clear, cool. The river was pale rusty brown, the color of potter's clay.

Pushing off into the flow I checked the map, though not because I had really expected to learn my location. It was a color-ful map of Ashland County, the kind given free to tourists. Paved and gravel roads were clearly marked but not the topography, and the scale was an imprecise three miles to the inch. On this map the White River appeared as a series of northeast-trending squiggles drawn with artistic flair. As the crow flies it is thirteen miles from the Highway 13 put-in to Odanah. But the winding route would probably put the river mileage over twenty—how far over I had no idea. I noticed from the map that a large stream called Hyms Creek joined the White from the south. If I found it, this confluence would mark roughly a third of the distance I was to travel.

The wind continued its gusting, shifting ways as I paddled along. Sometimes it drove the canoe into a bank or blasted so hard it pushed the boat back upstream. It was difficult to rest the paddle long enough to gaze at a thicket of wild plums or make notes. But if the tumultuous wind made work, it also brought an overwhelming sense of seasonal change. It was as if that day the atmosphere was turning over, much as deep lakes circulate their layer of cold water to the surface in autumn. With the shaking and swaying of limbs and spilling of leaves, with the migrating birds, I could even imagine the land itself was turning over.

As I continued along, the small details of my surroundings began to impress and inform me. From a strange-looking stand of short trees with big leaves strayed the voice of a chickadee, the first bird I had seen on the trip. A closer look found the trees to be leafless box elders heavily covered over with the "leaves" of wild grapes. A dragonfly caught my attention as it sputtered past. Little is known about these late-emerging river dragonflies, especially in this part of the state. Some of these may be rare species, perhaps not yet described for Wisconsin. Farther along, tracks of a mink on the prowl cut across a mud bar at a bend. Along the banks, ranks of tall asters gone to seed stood in front of legions of black ash. From a patch of red osier dogwood covering the sandy tongue of a bar at the next bend, a surprised robin flitted away.

The current seemed as if it had slowed, though I was not sure of this. On my right, a small but distinct stream entered the

White. In passing it I peered as far as I could up its narrow channel overarched with silver maples. Was this Hyms Creek? I could not be sure, but it was possible. Even good maps are only approximations of reality to begin with, and the map I had with me was at best someone else's guess of the present course of a river that took many millennia to get where it is. Hyms Creek or not, at this point it mattered little. It was a beautiful, intriguing stream and I promised myself to return someday to find it again.

On an older, which is to say higher, river terrace a stand of sugar maples blazed like a leafy inferno in the sunlight. Patches of wild plum and hawthorn topped the banks, with sedges swirled by wind beneath them. About three feet above the water's surface I noticed the sedges were all combed in the downstream direction and flattened against the bank. Low branches of trees and red osier hanging about the same level as the sedges were plastered with dead leaves. These were telltale signs that recently the White had been flowing even higher and faster than it was now. There is a small hydroelectric reservoir upriver, but it is doubtful that their releases could have caused this high flow. Regardless of where the flow came from it must have made for some wild water, even here on Old Man River.

Another bend, and then I saw something I hadn't noticed before. It was some kind of white oak, tilting far out over the river's edge at an angle that will not be tenable for much longer. A few of its heavy roots were exposed, curving like massive, clasping tendrils into the disintegrating clay bank. Some of its leathery leaves had already begun to change to a deep, rust-tinged yellow color. As the canoe swept beneath a drooping limb I snatched a leaf. The rounded lobe tips looked like fingers, and a pair of deep notches, or sinuses, almost met in the middle, up about a third its length from the stem. Memories of childhood downstate came sweeping back: this was a bur oak, the same great bur oaks once found in Wisconsin's extensive savannah landscape at the fringes of prairie. How unusual it was to find such a tree growing along the banks of a northern river. And how extraordinary to have found it in a region that some plant ecologists have classified as a boreal lowland. A hundred yards downriver I passed another bur oak, and then I saw more of them, each clutching the riverbank. I wondered how many I had already passed and carelessly mistaken for northern red oaks.

The bur oaks seemed strangely out of place to me, and I wondered if they were artifacts, the result of deliberate or accidental plantings by Ojibway or the earlier Sioux, or by *voyaguers*? The fur trading *couriers du bois* that traveled up the Mavaise (Ojibway for "Bad") River reported in their notes and journals that it could be canoed to its headwaters in Lake Owen. From there it was a short portage to Namekagon Lake and the St. Croix and Mississippi River systems, where bur oaks were common. Today most people know that Lake Owen is the headwaters not of the Bad River, but of the White River. The reason for this is that for a long time the White River didn't exist. On the old maps it appeared as one of two forks of the Bad River. It was much later that the well-traveled west fork came to be called the White River. This river route was, along with the Brule River route, one of the two water highways by which Native Americans, trappers, and traders alike made their way far inland.

Farther ahead I could see white cedar growing in tight clumps along the riverbank and near the bottom of hill slopes where rainwater collected in shallow clay pockets. Tall basswoods grew together there in clumps. They were actually clones regenerated from the same rootstock of a single tree that had been cut or broken off in a windstorm. The frost-nipped, drooping leaves of red osier dogwood looked like a purple haze on the banks.

At a bend a robin zipped across the river and into the armor of several big hawthorns. I eased the canoe onto a sandbar there, just to listen and watch. This resting place was well out of the wind, and I enjoyed the comfort it offered. From the direction of the thorns there came the trill of cedar waxwings. Arrowwood and blue vervain, now gone to seed, were growing nearby. A "chit" call told of a yellow-rumped warbler nearby. Too soon the river's current worked the canoe free from the sandbar, and like the leaves on the water I was adrift once again. Down we went, the leaves and me, the river carrying us together, the chaos of the current not telling us how far we would be carried, or when or where we would be deposited.

From the right another small feeder stream entered Old Man River, adding to the volume of its flow. In places basswood were becoming abundant and seemed to replace the silver maples. Ahead were big white spruces with clumps of alder growing beneath. A few bends more downstream and the canoe swerved around a large whirlpool, its vortex filled with leaves. Just beyond this, a big old paper birch had fallen across the river. It was the easiest portage I had so far.

Downstream, I paddled around bend after bend, sometimes working against the wind, sometimes driven by it. Once in a while it would get the best of me and spin the canoe around or drive it into a bank. Wood ducks appeared ahead but when they saw me they departed in haste upstream, squawking as they do. Juneberry, chokecherry, willow, sedge, joe-pye weed gone to seed. On I went, losing track of time to the stroke of the paddle, paddling and losing thoughts of elsewhere in the recognition and naming of everything I saw.

A sudden awakening came like a spark of electricity. As the canoe rounded a bend, far overhead I saw thick steel cables spanning the river. The current carried me beneath them, and I saw the towers that supported the high voltage lines. A wide swath had been cut through the forest, and down it ran the power lines like a suture over a great gash. Before long it was behind me, yet something had been lost in passing those lines. From that point I could not quite see the river as it had been only minutes before. A measure of the wildness of this river country had been stripped away forever.

The wind there took a new bite, and paddling became more difficult. My knees began to ache from kneeling in the canoe, and my arms were growing weary. The trip was no longer a joy ride, but had become strenuous work. How much farther I had to go was unknown, but the sun was getting closer to the horizon and I set my mind to the task of paddling.

Soon, my halting paddle strokes settled into an easier rhythm. The canoe forged ahead, despite the pommeling of the strong, shifting winds. Downriver I went, not thinking much about the river or anywhere else. Like the old *voyageurs* my mind was on the water, on the snags and sandbars, on the lookout for the telltale ripples running toward me which provided at least a few seconds to prepare for a strong gust of wind. This time, as I passed an ugly riprapped area where a gas main dove below the river, I barely took notice. Paddling and moving with the water were all that concerned me then.

On stretches where I could paddle more or less with the wind, I sat on the canoe seat to give my knees a rest. When the wind wasn't gusting there was time to notice ruby-crowned kinglets feeding in white spruce, to see a kingfisher secret away downstream. Silver maples. Box elder. Sedges tossed in the wind that made a hissing sound. Dry leaves that rattled and fell. The canoe passed beneath a basswood that arched low over the water. Then a gust hit and sent me slowly spinning downstream. A spooked heron jumped from the bank, then struggled momentarily as it gained altitude before racing away downstream on a tailwind.

When the canoe was on a stretch of river running west or northwest, or when spurious gusts surprised me from other directions, I knelt and paddled with as much gusto as I could muster. As I passed beneath another power line, and then yet another, I barely noticed. I had found a strange serenity in the midst of chaos. All the world around me was in flux, paddling against the wind was difficult, and the power and gas corridors were a dark smudge on this otherwise wild country. Yet the trip so far had been wonderful. I realized there was nothing I could do about the wind or the wires. So I let those troubles go.

The canoe was pulled along by the current, swept downstream with all the lost leaves, branches, and detritus of Old Man River. I got on my knees again, but this time in devotion to wind and water. Then I grabbed the paddle and began stroking the river for all I was worth.

The rhythm of the river ran through me again. Bend, run, bend, paddle hard, bend, run. Almost as if in a dream the tour proceeded, the river miles receded. I never thought about distance again or counting bends. My measure of progress was strange. I tried to notice everything as I paddled by. Clusters of swamp milkweed; shining yellow-top, pale yellow-bottom silver maple leaves, crinkled where they mingled with the sedges along the shore; touching soft silver maple leaves as I passed beneath a low branch; feeling how the air cools fast whenever fast-moving clouds obscure the sun; an abandoned chickenwire trap mangled in a logjam; poison ivy glowing red on the banks; already leafless black ash trees standing together nakedly; elderberries; a yellow-rumped warbler that chits and dashes away; a raven that cruises over, eyes me suspiciously, croaks once, and flies on.

Slowly, but not quite imperceptibly, the character of the terrain changes. Once the river seemed to meander tightly between high clay valley walls. Now it ran in wider curves with longer reaches between bends. Even the hills had receded, leaving only a few solitary mounds for the river to run against. The land on either side of the river had taken on the character of a large bottom land, a wide, flat flood plain terrace that flooded often. Here side streams entered the river as deep "V" notches that cut through the sheer, steep riverbank.

Around a bend there was yet another logjam blocking passage. I found a place to pull the boat up the steep eight-foot bank and then dragged it through impossibly dense brush around the jam. On the other side the banks had been cut nearly vertical, and the only place I could find to put the canoe in was a straight drop of ten feet. By luck I got the boat back in the water without swamping it, then climbed down the trunk and branches of a fallen silver maple to lower myself in the boat.

Downstream, the largest stands of white cedar I had seen so far on this trip appeared on the banks. There were also big stands of shiny, white paper birch, with brilliant yellow leaves that shimmered in the sunshine. There was a spicy aroma in the air, an odor I recognized as sedges and sweet gale in a marsh. A hairy woodpecker hammered away at a dead elm, then bolted away as I passed by.

A woodcock burst from a muddy hollow along the shore. From the lay of the land I could tell that I was definitely on the flats here. The wind above was roaring, but, having no hills to ricochet from or steep valley corridors to follow, it presented trouble mostly when the river headed in a westerly direction. Old Man River was much broader here, and seemed to meander with the greatest leisure.

At some point I realized that it had gotten very late in the day. I was surprised to see the sun had sunk so low that I could not see it behind the trees. How much farther I yet had to go was uncertain. Not far, I told myself. Sitting silently in the canoe, I listened for sounds from the world of people. When the wind hushed for a few seconds, I could hear in the distance the familiar whine of truck tires on pavement. The truck must have been on the highway to the north. How far away I couldn't tell, but I guessed a mile or two at most.

Paddling along quickly, I read the last pages of the book that is Old Man River country. Many large, twiggy nests in a stand of black ash just beyond the west bank told of a heron rookery. Large clusters of basswood spoke of ancestor trees that once stood in the same place. Fireweed, blue vervain, and joe-pye weed on a low bank hinted of silt laid down in recent years. The inside corner of a bend that was overgrown with hog peanut strongly suggested that they had been planted here by the Ojibway. Elsewhere, nodding woodland sunflower heads, common milkweed, and sweet gale spoke only of themselves.

The river continued to broaden, and sounds from the highway were continuously heard. The wind was still blowing the canoe about like a bathtub toy at times. As I approached old Odanah, I was overwhelmed with the richness of the river. I stopped to sample chokecherries—tart, yet delicious made into jelly. As I shoved off from shore, a mink ran along the bank to where I had landed the canoe. There it stopped briefly and sniffed in my direction before disappearing in the sedges. Wild grapes weighted down the branches of small trees and shrubs and hung like thick ropes from the limbs of taller trees. I tasted a handful of grapes, which were not very sweet but dry and delicious in their own way. Virginia creeper twined in the trees where grapes were absent. Around a bend a coot appeared and then tried to dive but popped back to the surface like a cork. Then it ran and flapped its small wings as it struggled to take flight. A small school of minnows jumped from the water, but I could not see the big fish that pursued them.

I drifted by a hawthorn full of bright red fruit, its thorny armament hard to see from the water. Ostrich ferns grew lushly here in stretches on the clay banks, as they have elsewhere along the river.

By now the wind had lost much of its intensity and within an hour would be reduced to a breeze.

Rounding the thousandth bend I heard dogs barking, and saw a few old cars parked near a house trailer. This, I realized, was old Odanah. I paddled along quietly, passing the old motorboats tied up at the pier behind the trailer. An ice shanty on wooden runners at the river's edge waited for winter.

Beyond the house the river quickly widened as it joined the larger Bad River running from the south. The sun had already set as I paddled between the concrete piers which once supported a train trestle, and then I turned the canoe sharply east. Through the twilight I passed old Odanah, beyond the Methodist church, beyond the old Indian school, beyond patches of wild rice and the small houses and quiet noises of the reservation. By the time I reached the boat landing the sky was already darkening. I unfolded sore legs and stepped stiffly ashore. After carrying the canoe to a grassy place, I tipped it and placed my paddle and life preserver beneath it. Then, walking as briskly as I could, I headed for the highway where I would have to hitch a ride to the nearest phone booth so I could call Julie to come pick me up.

On the highway I started walking as I hitchhiked. When I came to the bridge over the Bad River, I stopped and gazed awhile at the river, thinking of the long haul I had come and all that I had seen. This was the day I had floated with the leaves down through the wild heart of Old Man River country.

WHITE ON WHITE

Several years ago, it seemed the inhabitants of Lake Superior country were headed for one of those hard winters old-timers always talk about. In early October, unseasonable snow showers had been dusting field and forest with primer coats of white. It was as if the land were trying winter on for size early this year to see if it might fit. Birds offered further evidence of impending conditions. Migrating ducks and geese had been arriving early, yet they spent little time feeding in the coastal bays and marshes before moving on. Most of the nesting songbirds had already taken wing, leaving behind a few late-migrating fox sparrows, song sparrows, and juncos to linger among the resident birds. Most impressive of all were the flocks of snow buntings, down early this year from their distant Canadian nesting grounds. Some of them had not yet fully molted their fancy "black and white tux" breeding plumage. For a few weeks they could easily be seen in fields and on beaches and roadsides where they searched for seed and grit.

The old folks in town were also talking snow, giving a nod or look that said, "We've seen this before." Their faces, weathered with experience, possessed a certain infallibility about the matter. In a vague way they knew fairly well what was coming. And

besides, it was all right there in the *Old Farmer's Almanac.* Who could question that?

By early November, the weather was indeed more wintry. By that time the ground had already frozen deep enough that the snow could begin accumulating. It seemed that a climatic point of no return had been passed. The snow would continue to fall, and it would not melt again in any significant way until the next spring. The white-tailed deer were already well into the mating season, which annoyed some hunters because three weeks remained until the deer rifle season would open. Other hunters were glad to see the snow, which would make seeing and tracking deer easier. Those of us who like to ski were of course pleased. Most everyone in town seemed to have an opinion about the weather which they wanted to voice.

Winter is not taken lightly here in the north. To have snow on the ground and long, cold nights for almost a third of the year— from early November well into March—is no small matter. For some people, cabin fever and other cold-dark-season maladies set in shortly after the holidays end. We must sympathize with those for whom spring seems impossibly distant and winter a hardship that must be endured. Yet many of us live or have moved here by choice. We came because we found the land and lake beautiful and interesting. Now our lives have grown into this place as deeply as the roots of an old white pine. We have found life in the North Coast country meaningful and endlessly fascinating. Our own sense of place here has been gleaned not only from pages of history, but from our own daily encounters and adventures with the land and lake. Berry picking or ice fishing, painting pictures or shoveling snow. In these and countless other ways we have come to find that we are at home here, not just in summer but in every season. Certainly, winter presents its share of inconveniences and problems. Clenched in the icy fangs of late January, one would have to be subhuman not to grumble and complain in some measure. But most of us here have learned how to stay warm and enjoy the best of winter.

About the second week of December, the ice on Chequamegon Bay had frozen to a thickness of about two inches. People were already walking out on the new ice and fishing a few hundred yards offshore from the DNR boat landing at the S-curve on Highway 13. Within days rumors were floating around that the trout were so hungry that one had been caught on a bare hook. True or not, the rumors were yet other incarnations of the proverbial carrot on a stick. So a few days later, with tip-ups and jigging rod in a backpack, a dozen lake shiners in a pickle bucket, and my trusty ice chisel in hand to probe with, I ventured forth onto the unknown.

To walk out on fresh ice just thick enough to support one's weight is to be either a fool or fully awakened to the present moment, to the possibilities of living and dying. Carefully shuffling out on ice as clear as glass, I could see bottom perfectly, and imagined that I was walking on air. The water was not yet deep enough there to drown a body. As I walked farther, the sand and gravel bottom gave way to cobbles, and soon these seemed to descend beneath my boots into an eerie darkness. It was a place I had no intention of visiting this season.

The ice was firm enough to hold me, though in a couple of places it seemed to bend, and loud "cracks" shot away in different directions from my feet. In about twenty feet of water the ice was no worse, though I could see the south wind was rippling open water only a hundred yards away. The fish were supposed to be "jumping out of the holes," so I quickly set two tip-ups with shiners and then started jigging a small Swedish pimple baited with a little salmon spawn. It was not long before I caught a nice splake on a tip-up, and I thought that maybe under thin ice conditions one fish would suffice. But then the other tip-up flag sprang up and this time I caught a twenty-some-inch brown trout. I recall thinking how delectable the fish would be filleted and marinated in olive oil, garlic, shoyu, and sherry, then broiled on foil and served with home-made tartar sauce, Julie's café potatoes, and chilled glasses of some good white zinfandel. I could have magnanimously let these fish go, but they are not native to Lake Superior. The DNR stocks splake and brown trout specifically to be caught and presumably eaten. I had to do my duty.

That brown was motivation enough to keep jigging for a few more minutes. But I had not been at it long when I was startled by a sound like lightning striking nearby and jolted from my throne on the pickle bucket. Luckily, I didn't break through the ice. But the crashing sound and jolt, that troubled me. It could have been that another sheet of ice had been shifted by the wind and crashed into the one I was on. Or maybe the current was pulling this ice sheet away from shore. Either way, I had no desire to be stranded on a piece of thin ice. Hastily I packed the fish and my gear, and cautiously walked ashore.

No one likes to stop and go home while the fish are biting, including me. But I was comforted when I recalled a maxim and corollary of an old gentleman I once met fishing out on the coal dock. He said, "Over the long haul, cowards will catch more fish." His corollary was, "If you drown, you won't catch any fish." With that in mind, I headed home to fillet and sauté the catch *du jour*.

For most of the winter ice fishing isn't a very perilous pastime on the bay because of ice conditions. It is the weather here that can be far more treacherous. Subzero temperatures, ferocious wind chill, and white-out conditions—these are ever-present considerations that should be taken seriously by anyone who would venture out on the lake or in the woods under marginal conditions. While driving home, I thought of the first Europeans to overwinter in this region and how they dealt with the weather. I thought of them because they built the first known non-Indian dwelling in the area. Their little fort was said to have been located near the head of the bay, a few miles to the south of where I had been fishing.

The year was 1659, and the first white men to visit this area were Medard Chouart Des Groseilliers and Pierre Esprit Radisson.

They were French explorers and entrepreneurs from Quebec who had paddled a sturdy birch-bark canoe up the Saint Lawrence River and northwest through three great lakes. The Ojibway people may have first discovered them when they portaged the rapids of the Saint Mary's River and entered Lake Superior. From there, they traveled along the south shore of the lake. Eventually they arrived at a large Ojibway village located at a place now known as La Pointe, on Madeline Island.

That autumn, Radisson and Groseilliers traveled four days with the Ojibway to another large village at a site near present-day Lac Court Oreilles. There they endured a most horrendous winter with the Ojibway and other tribes that had arrived there. Radisson wrote in his journal that he and Groseilliers had nearly starved and frozen to death that winter. Unable to kill game because the snow was too deep to support a hunter on snowshoes, Radisson wrote that their condition "grows wors and wors daily." "First we did eate or dogs," he wrote. Later they retraced their steps into the woods and were "glad to get the bones and carcasses of the beast we had killed earlier." Finally, in great desperation they ate "boiled skins, ground bones and tree bark."

Radisson gravely wrote of the Native Americans encamped at Lac Court Oreilles, "here are above 500 dead. It's time to come out of such miseryes." They had died of starvation, cold, and disease. Radisson did not write about the matter again. Perhaps he could find no words to explain the depths of human pain and suffering that had taken place there that hard winter.

By comparison, our own problems with winter are trivial, and the risks we take are frivolous and of our own choosing. It is important to consider that this was not always so.

It was a Saturday afternoon in late January, and snow conditions for cross-country skiing had been quite good so far that winter. The day looked promising, so Julie and I had bundled up the kids and taken them skiing, as we often do, on the groomed forest service trails at Valhalla. The area was once used as an Olympic training center for the U.S. Nordic team in the 1930s. Now trees have reclaimed most of the area, except for the steep ski jump hill and landing area which remain intact. Fresh snow had fallen recently, and it was a beautiful, almost clear-sky day. The wax we used was "Green Extra," which translates to an air temperature of about seventeen or eighteen degrees. The skiing conditions would be excellent.

The kids, Jessie and Casey, had a few seasons of skiing behind them and eagerly took off down the trail. It is one of the great pleasures of parenting to watch your children thoroughly enjoying an activity or sport that you have cherished for many years. By the time our kids are in high school, they will be competent, if not expert, skiers. But for now it's great fun to just herringbone up hills, stop to look at oak leaves or eat snow, look for footprints of deer or fox, fly down hills and sometimes crash—our kids know what skinny skiing is all about. We see it as a kind of gift we can share with them, yet another way to help them be happy and healthy throughout their lives.

That day we were skiing a hilly three-mile loop. Finally we found ourselves atop the last big hill. From there it was mostly downhill for the last half mile, the trail leveling off near the beautiful old CCC log cabin now used as a warming hut. The hill starts down as a fast, sweeping drop that requires snow plowing to avoid taking the curve too fast and crashing. After that there is another shorter, steep drop, and then a very long, easy glide almost back to the cabin. Mom went first, followed by Jessie, then Casey, and then me. The kids skied the hill perfectly. When I caught up with them I realized that this was the first time all of us made it down without crashing. The hill had always been the one big challenge for the kids. But now they had skied it and we knew that they were ready for longer trails and higher hills. Traveling the winter hills and exploring the white world had become second nature for Jessie and Casey, as we always hoped it would.

Only weeks later, in February, I heard rumors about snowy owls showing up in our area. The first of these discoveries came up in small talk overheard in the check-out line at the Washburn IGA. A woman there was talking about this big bird perched atop a silo just outside of town. I see it every time I drive by there, she said. My ears perked. The check-out clerk ventured that it was some kind of hawk. No, I don't think so, she continued. No, it looked kind of like an owl or something, and it was white. Unable to restrain myself, I blurted out, "It's a snowy owl!" The women looked at me strangely, then abruptly changed their conversation to another topic. But I had a good idea where that silo was. After paying for the groceries, I drove a half mile north from town and there was the owl. It was perched right where the woman said it would be.

With binoculars I was able to get a good look at this stoic winter visitor. I whistled and the owl twisted its head toward me in that strange, hyper-extended way only owls can do. Beneath slightly drooping eyelids the snowy's warm yellow eyes gazed indifferently in my direction. Its feathers were mostly white, though above its eyes and on its sides and wings there was some black flecking. Had this bird set down in a snowy field or out on the ice, as they sometimes do, like the Cheshire Cat it would have mysteriously disappeared save for its eyes and flecks. But the presence of the owl here was an even greater mystery.

A few days later my friend Joan told me the whereabouts of another owl, so I drove over to the beach at the head of the bay in Ashland to see if I could find it. With binoculars I scanned the rough, snow-covered ice for more than a half hour and was about ready to leave when I finally found the snowy. I had searched the same area repeatedly, yet I could not see the owl because it had blended so well with the irregular, snow-covered ice. White on white, cold and snow, the hardship of winter, the will to survive. The snowy owl seemed to embody the very essence of winter. I wondered why this bird was just setting out on the ice of the bay. The thought crossed my mind that perhaps it felt more like home there.

A week or two later, I learned that snowy owls and other far northern owls like great gray, hawk, and boreal owls had been reported across northwestern Wisconsin and central Minnesota. In fact, many emaciated dead owls had been found, which suggests they starved to death.

Normally these northern owls prefer to remain on their home territories during winter. Depending on the species, "home" could be anywhere from northern Minnesota's boreal forests to the Canadian arctic tundra. But when food is unavailable—when lemmings or snowshoe hares or ptarmigan are at the low point in their population cycles, or when unusually heavy snow cover makes capturing prey next to impossible—the owls must look elsewhere or starve.

It seems likely that those snowy owls I saw were here for the same reasons. Doubtless the snowy ensconced atop the silo had chanced upon a good supply of farm rodents. It remained in the area until the weather began to warm up at the end of the month. The snowy owl on the ice was gone within a week. One could only hope that it did not meet the same fate as the other owls that had been found.

White on white, eating or starving, risk upon risk, freezing or warming, and chance upon chance, living or dying. In every corner of the North Coast country the dramas of life in winter are played out. It is the great good fortune of those of us living here at this time to be able to partake of the wonders of winter, and to survive them. But it was not always this way.

OLD COPPER

I t was years ago that I drove to Steve Dunker's antique and what-not shop on Siskiwit Bay in Cornucopia to return a book I had borrowed months before (he has since moved his business to Washburn). Steve remembered me immediately. He is a literate fellow, with a wry wit that probably sails right over many of his patrons. Old books, antiques, and found things are his passions. He is also a most remarkable entrepreneur.

As I perused his natural history books, I overheard him comment to a woman admiring a large painted chest of drawers that he had raised the price on it considerably only last week when someone tried to buy it. The chest was solid walnut, he said, and he didn't want to part with it until he had the chance to refinish it and see the beauty of the piece for himself. I'm not going to let this baby slip away so easy, is the gist of what he said. And he didn't.

Steve's store was intriguing because all kinds of interesting things seemed to turn up there. To find a very old Cambridge reprint of Charles Darwin's *Origin of Species* on his shelves was a real surprise. Behind me an ecstatic elderly woman was buying an armload of prints she had searched far and wide for in the Twin Cities. There was no telling what might be found there.

I continued scanning titles, and found a book about Native American artifacts that held my attention for some time. When I felt a tap on my shoulder I turned to find Steve holding up what looked like a palm-sized, dark brownish-gray stone with some crusty flecks of green here and there on it. The surface was smooth and very finely pitted, and its shape was odd—sort of an elongated rectangle in outline and somewhat rounded across its length, thicker in the middle than at the ends.

He asked me what I thought it was. It looked and felt like a very heavy rock, maybe a chunk of iron formation that had been carried in a glacial streambed.

But then I noticed the scratch: the metal beneath glinted copper like electrical wire. A piece of native copper? I asked. He said it was sort of that, but asked me to turn it over.

I hefted the stone over into my other hand and saw on the underside two opposite edges that were folded back over, obviously by intention, into narrow ridges nearly the length of the object. Viewed on end these ridges formed a tall, narrow "C" that could clasp the tapered end of a flattened stick. The other end was tapered as if it once had been sharp. It seemed the object was a crude tool, perhaps the tip of an ice spud. But copper?

Steve grinned and pulled a book off the shelf with a bookmark in it. He flipped to the marked page and on it was a photograph of three objects that were almost identical to the one I held in my hand. Then he held up the book to show the title: *Artifacts of Native America.*

Steve looked me straight in the eye and said that it was an adze head pounded from native copper. It was definitely Old Copper Culture, at least three thousand years old and maybe as old as seven thousand years.

The object—the adze head—grew heavier as the meaning of his words set in. It seemed to buzz with a strange power of its own.

Where did you get this?, I asked. From a guy with a metal detector who sells him pieces of float copper he occasionally finds. Float copper is a piece of native copper that was carried and deposited by the continental glacier that once covered this area. Pieces of it have occasionally been found in fields and streams throughout the area. Steve thought the man might have found this piece nearby, but he honestly didn't know.

My mind reeled and shivers ran down my spine. I held that adze head tightly, letting its significance take hold of me. Here was a tool that some person or persons crafted thousands of years ago while my ancestors in Europe were still using stones and bones. In my hand was tangible evidence of one of the early milestones of human development—the ability to extract a native metal and form it into a tool.

The adze head seemed all the more significant because it wasn't found far away. It was found somewhere nearby, perhaps closer than we realized. This too belonged to one of the ancient peoples who were the distant forbearers of the modern Woodland Indians, and perhaps of the Ojibway people who live here now.

I was curious to find out who the person was who found the copper adze so I could ask him where he had found it. Steve said that, for reasons unknown, this guy asked him not to reveal his name if people inquired about the adze. He thought it was a strange request, but a promise was a promise. I knew Steve was a very honest person, so I let the matter rest right there. But I was still fascinated by the idea of people living in this region thousands of years ago. Who were they and how did they live? What did they do in winter?

Previously, I had not found a single book in the local libraries containing information about the paleo-history of this region. Yet here was what seemed to be hard evidence that an ancient people lived in, or at least passed through, the area. Weeks later, after a trip to the Northland College library to learn more about the Copper Culture, I called Dr. Robert Birnbaum, the state archeologist, in Madison. I wanted information about archeological "digs" in northwestern Wisconsin, and hopefully some references for reports from nearby studies.

Dr. Birnbaum's news was not encouraging. There had been only a few digs in this entire region, and none of them in Bayfield County. The only other record of an ancient copper artifact in this area that he knew of had recently been found in a pile of soil from a building excavation in Bayfield.

Despite this uneventful news, I felt sure paleolithic people had been here and that more evidence had to be around. I was also discouraged that so little professional archeological work had been done in the area.

After mulling on this for almost a year, it seemed the only people in this area who would know the whereabouts of copper artifacts, if there were any, would be local metal detector buffs. So for a few weeks I ran an ad in the local newspaper that I hoped would catch their attention, particularly the guy who found the adze.

Much to my disappointment, not one person called. I ran the ad again later with the same result. Still unwilling to accept defeat, I began questioning detector-toting treasure hunters wherever I found them. None knew, or were willing to concede they knew, of any copper artifacts having been found on the Bayfield Peninsula. Stumped again after a summer of trying, I conceded defeat.

By the time the following spring arrived I had all but forgotten about the adze. Then one Saturday I went shorecasting up the coast a ways at a favorite place I call Poet's Ledge. Two hours and two nice brown trout later, I saw a man with a metal detector who was obviously working the cliff edge.

When he drew near, we pleasantly spoke about fishing for a while before I turned the conversation to copper artifacts. He stoically said that he had once found what he later believed to be a copper knife, but that he had thrown it out into the lake. Otherwise, he said, no copper. But his change from a casual demeanor to a sudden poker face when I asked about copper led me to believe otherwise. I gave him my business card and asked him to call me if he ever ran into the person I was looking for. He said he sure would, and with that he hustled off and was gone.

A few months later I received a phone call in the middle of a weekday afternoon. The male voice sounded nervous, but vaguely familiar. It was the man I had met at Poet's Ledge and, yes, the one who sold Steve the copper adze. To protect his anonymity, I'll just call him John.

John is a regular fellow who lives in the Chequamegon Bay area and works for a local manufacturer. He told me that he had been treasure hunting for a number of years. He liked to work the beaches and places along the shore where he might find older, more interesting items like pieces of native copper or coins from the last century. Usually he finds very little, but once in a while he comes up with something unusual.

Several years ago John had been treasure hunting in a new area when he found the adze head "almost at the surface." He knew it was copper but had no idea what it was, so he sold it as a curiosity to Steve. Not long after he found a few other copper objects that looked like spear points up the shore close to Bayfield. He did a little research of his own and learned that the copper pieces he had found were artifacts that might be thousands of years old.

John also provided second-hand information about another man, now deceased, who years ago had found a large number of

copper artifacts, including a copper headdress and other orna-
mentation, somewhere south of Bayfield. He had no idea what
became of these.

It was a couple of months later when I heard from John
again. I asked to see the artifacts he had collected, and one day he
brought an assortment to my house. There spread on our kitchen
table were what looked like a knife blade, a spear point, a couple
of awls, several other pieces that may have been arrowheads, and
one that might have been a fishhook. Coated with a heavy greenish oxide, they looked every bit as ancient as they were.

Later John brought me along to look at several of the areas
where he found artifacts. To my eyes they looked like absolutely
ordinary coastal woods, except for their proximity to the shoreline.
The ages have worn away any trace of encampments or villages.
There was no telling what had or had not been there.

It was about this same time that John contacted the state
archeologist's office with very high hopes of exciting some interest in archeological research here. He told me that Dr. Birnbaum
himself visited these sites with him, but found nothing that would
merit an archeological survey in the foreseeable future.

So the central mystery remains: Who were these people
who made and used copper tools?

Their adzes could have been used to construct sturdy
shelters or make fine dugout canoes, as was done in the Pacific
Northwest. Copper fishhooks, arrowheads, spear points, and knives

suggest a high level of technical refinement that must have pervaded every aspect of their lives. As hunters and fishers they probably lived well. The headdress seems emblematic of the importance of culture, spirituality, and ceremony in their lives. But this is only my guess. It is extremely difficult to infer any more than this.

We can be certain of only one thing. Before Europeans came, before the Ojibway and the Lakota who came before them— far, far back in the receding light of time, there were people here. They knew how to take copper from rock and use it in a way that had never been done before. They were the ancient ones.

IN PRAISE OF
YELLOW BIRCH

For some years now I have been harboring a grudge that indirectly concerns paper birches. Recently this grudge came to mind again while rifle hunting for deer in a relatively youthful forest here in Bayfield County.

Near a favorable intersection of deer trails I found a charred, sawed-off old pine butt ideally positioned with a paper birch for a back rest; someone had obviously hunted there before.

Sitting quietly, I soon observed that most of the trees in this forest were paper birches, along with a scattering of smaller fir and red pines. Dense stands of paper birch such as this are often found on drier, sandier soils. They also arise where intense fires have burned the topsoil away. Sometimes these intense burns happened in older, more mature woods as the result of dry conditions and lightning strikes. But more often they were the result of accidental or deliberate slash fires following clearcutting.

As most older residents will recall, there have been many fires throughout the north country—including here in Bayfield County—especially in the first half of this century. Those fires are where many of these pure paper birch stands got their start. Like aspen, paper birch are a pioneer species, often the first to appear in a forest or abandoned field.

This is the ecological role of paper birches; they are just doing what comes naturally, only more so in recent history because of human-caused changes in the forests.

Paper birches are lovely trees, even more picturesque when seen together in a pure stand. And there is a certain amount of romance associated with their use in former times by the Ojibway and other tribes in the making of medicines, birch bark canoes, lodges, baskets, and other implements. It's easy to see why they appear in so many paintings, on sweatshirts, and in or on items at craft shows. People practically adore paper birches.

Now I have to confess that I also happen to feel that paper birches are beautiful and interesting. And though I didn't see a single deer that chilly day, I enjoyed immensely the serene purity of that paper birch stand, the sound of the white November winds soughing through those living limbs.

But as much as I admire paper birches, after thinking about them a little while, they sooner or later led my thoughts back in time. And that's where the grudge comes in.

As I said, this grudge is nothing personal against paper birches themselves. It's just that, in a sad way, they remind me of another kind of birch and a different kind of forest that once predominated across northern Wisconsin and Michigan. Sometimes I am taken by the same feeling just sitting in our house. You see, much of the woodwork and doors in our house is made of a beautiful, absolutely clear golden-hued birch milled back around 1919. But the wood is not paper birch.

Rather, it is from a tree whose name seems to have pretty much dropped out of the local vernacular. The tree I am talking about is yellow birch.

Before the era of the Great Cutover and railroad logging, before Scandinavian homesteaders came to start a new life here, and earlier still before the forests were "high graded" for white pine, giant yellow birches over a hundred feet tall and three feet in diameter were commonplace in our forests. Yellow birch was a vital part of a type of forest ecologists call the white pine-hemlock-yellow birch community.

Before the logging era, it was one of the most—if not *the* most—extensive forest types in Wisconsin. A vast, nearly unbroken tract of it once swept east from here all the way to New England.

Michigan's Porcupine Mountains hold fifty thousand or so acres of old-growth, much of it the original white pine-hemlock-yellow birch forest. Between the Sylvania Wilderness near Waters-meet and the private holdings of the Huron Mountain Club there is roughly another twenty-five thousand acres of these ancient forests.

Here in Wisconsin the only sizeable chunk of old-growth white pine-hemlock-yellow birch forest is found on the sovereign lands of the Menominee Indian Reservation. Tribal members there continue to log these forests selectively and with great care to maintain an intact and diverse old-growth ecological community. In so doing they practice a remarkable kind of restraint that is borne out of a concern for the life of the forest and for the future of their children. It is an uncommon form of stewardship that is seldom seen practiced elsewhere in America.

Aside from the Menominee tract, few old-growth forests of any kind remain in Wisconsin. These stands are small, isolated, and usually hard to find or reach. The wonderful two-hundred-acre old-growth remnant near the north end of Outer Island is among the largest of these. Facts of this kind are at the very heart of my grudge.

Here in Wisconsin, yellow birches remain a part of our forests today, though nowhere as abundant and rarely as large as they once were. Our old-growth forests are gone. Virtually all of them. The very end came when the north half of Outer Island was logged in the 1950s and early 1960s by the Lullabye Company. The wood was to be used to manufacture baby furniture.

My grudge, you see, is with the past. What galls me so deeply is that, unlike leaders of the Menominee tribe, out of the millions of acres of primal Wisconsin forest, no one in the first half of this century—no politicians or civic leaders or advocacy groups or individuals—had enough foresight, or concern for future generations, to save even a mere thirty or forty thousand acres of pristine forest. It seems that only lucre and greed prevailed; the evidence of this is everywhere around us.

But woods are woods, wildness is wildness, and we have what we have. We must move on. And so wherever I go in the big outside, I gratefully celebrate the wildness and diversity in our woods that has withstood more than a hundred years of deprivation. And in those lucky places in the landscape where I chance to find a few large yellow birch, hemlock, and white pines standing together, I have come to realize there is yet hope for the forests—and for our heirs—in the future.

Advances in the science of conservation biology over the past two decades have shed light on the importance of maintaining biological and genetic diversity and how we must think and act on a much larger "landscape scale" in order to protect the local diversity of our forests and wildlife. Conservation biologists will readily admit that a great deal remains to be understood about the complex web of interactions within a forest and between distant forests.

Yet already a sufficient set of ecosystem management principles has emerged that is guiding ecosystem managers and forest restorationists in other states as they take their first tentative steps in the centuries-long process of ecological restoration.

The restoration of a large tract of forest to an old-growth condition could someday begin right here in northern Wisconsin and, I must add, without significantly affecting the wood products industry. It will take public advocacy, political leadership, and a great deal of foresight and fortitude. But it can and should be done. For the yellow birch and for our children and their great-great-grand-children, it must be done.

ON THE TRAIL
OF WOLVES

Wolves were on my mind once again. A few days earlier my old fishing friend Tom had told me of his encounter with a wolf out in the national forest, and that's what got me thinking about them again.

Tom and his partner, Andrea, live in a place that is situated more or less southeast of Grandview, perhaps closer to Atkins Lake than not, give or take a handful of miles. They enjoy a level of solitude that only such a remote and vaguely defined place can offer. Their nearest neighbor is maybe five miles away, and it is a good three-mile drive to their mailbox. Those who are vaguely familiar with this neck of the woods might be tempted to say Tom and Andrea live in the middle of nowhere. But, as they would tell you themselves, they really live in the middle of everything.

Their forty acres of land is an inholding within the Chequamegon National Forest. It was once a frost-pocket homestead where a Swedish immigrant family eked out a heartache living. The land today is surrounded on all sides by miles and miles of trees. Fortunately, wild things are transparent to such human artifices as property and boundaries. Life moves freely in and

through their land and reveals itself in every season. Bear and deer, sugar maples and balsam fir, white-throated sparrows and spring peepers, mosquitoes and no-see-ums graciously share this place with Tom and Andrea.

Other than an occasional logging truck or a stray fisherperson motoring along the gravel road, there is little human activity in what amounts to a very large piece of wild country. In other words, the area is perfectly suited for wolves.

Wolves were one of the common interests that led to my friendship with Tom. One of our first adventures together was searching for signs of wolves that had been reported in the vicinity of the South Branch of the White River, not all that far from Delta. It was a Saturday afternoon in January, now years ago already, and we had been snowshoeing for hours without finding so much as a single paw print or piece of wolf scat. Tom thought it might be a good idea to drive south to the Rainbow Lake Wilderness and try there. Wolves had also recently been reported in that area and we thought we might try "howling" for them, hoping they would perhaps reciprocate our benevolent gestures.

First, we had to backtrack to Tom's truck, which was a couple of miles distant. Tom thought we could save time getting there if we forded the South Branch, which is spring fed and almost always open in winter. So we did, minus boots and socks, and with our pants and long underwear rolled as high as we could get them. We crossed at the shallowest riffle we could find, first throwing our boots and snowshoes over to a low bank on the other side. There was no turning back.

The water was knee-deep and colder than a well-digger's knee, like glacial meltwater only clearer and colder. Hollering and whooping in pain, we hotfooted up the snow-covered bank and wasted no time in pulling our dry socks and boots on before our toes froze.

An hour later we found ourselves howling for wolves over at Rainbow Lake; we sounded pitiful at first, but improved somewhat with practice. In the past, Tom had called wolves in other places and on occasion heard them reply. But wolves just weren't in the cards for us that day. Still, it had been a good beginning for a friendship.

For a few years after that small adventure, my thoughts turned to wolves only now and then, piqued by stories in newspapers and magazines and on the public radio airwaves. But then on a steely cold afternoon in early November my interest in wolves was rekindled in a more personal way.

Snow had fallen recently and I was driving far down untracked forest lanes to go bowhunting for deer from one of Tom's tree stands deep in the seemingly endless bog country around Clam Lake.

Proceeding slowly, I had just negotiated a sweeping bend when a very large, dog-like animal appeared as if out of thin air. It stood still there in the middle of the road, staring right at me. In the brief seconds it allowed me to look at it, I could see that, except for a few lighter markings about the eyes and muzzle, it had a thick, darkish—perhaps almost black—coat. It also held its head low as it stared, as if pausing to consider the insignificance of my presence. Then, as quickly as it had appeared, in an instant it bounded off the road into the spruce and tamarack.

I got out of the truck to look for footprints in the snow; they were the largest canine prints I had ever seen. I was many miles away from the nearest cabin and I knew this animal was no stray husky. Neither was it a coyote; the animal was far too large, the tracks much too big. I had already seen captive wolves, and of course many photos of them in books and magazines. The head and tail posture, the large body size, the thick muzzle, those intelligent eyes, and how my spine tingled. There was no doubt in my mind— I had just seen a wolf.

After that lucky chance encounter I began paying closer attention whenever I was out in the forest, tried to be more alert for wolf signs. Over the next few years I began to hear third-hand reports of wolf prints having been found—and even purported sightings of wolves—in the forests on the Bayfield Peninsula. In my heart I wanted to believe wolves had re-established themselves on the peninsula. Yet I found it hard to give much credence to what may have amounted to idle hearsay. And so a skeptic I remained, until this past December.

It was early in the month and I had been bowhunting for several weeks in a private forest above the Sioux River, miles from Washburn. Every evening about dusk I looked forward to being serenaded by the local coyote pack, sometimes accompanied by a barking red fox. As soon as the coyotes began to yip and howl, I always heard the local farm dogs far to the south join in the crooning.

But on this particular evening the coyotes were conspicuously silent. In fact the entire woods was quiet and all I could hear were the faint rumblings of heavy trucks moving along far-off Highway 13. Strangely, the small doe and two fawns that had frequented the apple bait did not show up either. There was an oddness to the silence, as if something were amiss in the woods. Maybe a bear was around, I guessed, or the deer had caught my scent—though they invariably snort when they do.

Finally, it was about ten minutes before hunting hours ended and the hunting situation was looking pretty bleak. And that's when it happened—one long, lone, hair-raising, spine-tingling, and not-very-distant howl.

The howl came from deeper in the woods, down in the direction of the river, from down the uncountable ages of the primal world. This was not the howl of a coyote or stray malamute. I had heard recordings of wolves howling many times before and *this one*, I knew and felt deep in my bones, was the howl of a wolf.

I waited quietly, shivering on my stand until dark, hoping to hear one more howl. But the woods remained dark and silent, and I walked out to my truck feeling about as lucky as a person can feel. Over the next year there were other reported signs and actual sightings of wolves. Finally, DNR biologists confirmed that a small pack of wolves had indeed taken up residence on the peninsula, and the Sioux River country was part of their territory.

It was not long after I heard the wolf howl that Tom had his own wolf story to tell. As I said earlier, the area where he lives is ideal wolf country. For a few weeks as he drove to work, he noticed what looked like large dog or coyote tracks in the snow along the road not far from his home. He didn't think much about them, but then one day he suddenly saw what had made the tracks.

Starting out for work as usual, just down the road from his driveway Tom had the rare good luck of seeing a wolf standing in plain view on the road. Tom is a dedicated biologist, but in all his wanderings in the woods and fields he had never seen a wolf in the wild. Until then. As with my wolf encounter, such a chance meeting, if not epiphanous, will at very least be etched in his memory forever. From that day on, whenever we are out in the big woods and bogs, along the unconscious edge of our awareness one wild question will run: Are there wolves here?

For decades wolves were demonized and persecuted throughout the United States. They were trapped, poisoned, and shot by bounty hunters right here in Wisconsin and neighboring states.

Now, after more than twenty years of difficult work restoring wolves to their former ranges and raising the public environmental conscience, it seems that wolves are ready to reveal themselves to us once again. If we can keep not just our eyes, but also our minds and hearts open, someday we will be ready—and worthy enough— to truly see wolves.

ABOUT THE AUTHOR

Michael Van Stappen lives with his family near the Wisconsin shores of Lake Superior. He is a naturalist writer who has found his own deep sense of place in Superior country through years of encounters and adventures with the lake and land. His stories have been featured in *Wisconsin Trails, Wisconsin Outdoor Journal, Bayfield County Journal,* and other regional and national publications.

ABOUT THE ILLUSTRATOR

Kate Wright, who lives in Cable, Wisconsin, is well known for her oil and watercolor works depicting the north country. She is also noted for her paintings on furniture, which have been shown at the Smithsonian Institution. Her work is included in collections throughout the United States.